STRATEGIES FOR writers

2

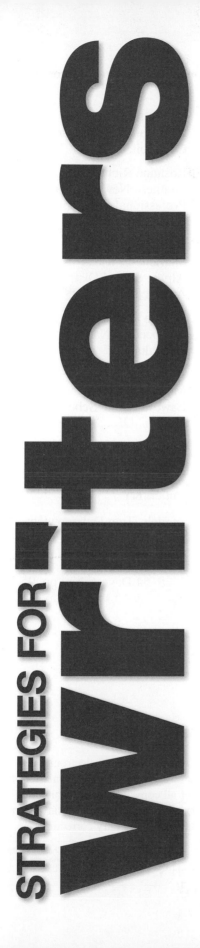

Senior Author

Rebecca Bowers Sipe, Ed.D.
Eastern Michigan University

Consulting Authors

Julie Coiro, Ph.D.
University of Rhode Island

Amy Humphreys, Ed.M., NBCT
Educational Consultant

Sara B. Kajder, Ph.D.
University of Pittsburgh

Mark Overmeyer, M.A.
Cherry Creek School District, Colorado

Senior Consultant

James Scott Miller, M.Ed.
National Writing Consultant

ZB Zaner-Bloser

Program Reviewers

Zaner-Bloser wishes to thank these educators who reviewed portions of this program and provided comments prior to publication.

Joe Anspaugh
Shelbyville Middle School
Shelbyville, IN

Michele Barto, Ed.D.
Fairleigh Dickinson University
Madison, NJ

Jackie Blosser
Lima City Schools
Lima, OH

Kim Bondy
South Arbor Academy
Ypsilanti, MI

Kelly Caravelli
Meadowbrook Middle School
Poway, CA

Cathy Cassy
St. Louis Public Schools
St. Louis, MO

Penny Clare
Educational Consultant
Lee, NH

Mary Dunton
Literacy Consultant
Sparks, NV

Emily Gleason
Beaverton School District
Beaverton, OR

Denise Gray, Ed.D.
Whiteriver Elementary School
Whiteriver, AZ

Laura Hall
Walton Charter Academy
Pontiac, MI

Donna Jett
Rockwood South Middle School
Fenton, MO

Christine Johnson, Ed.D.
Boonton Public Schools
Boonton, NJ

Dr. Roma Morris
Columbia School District
Columbia, MS

Rosanne Richards
Southern Nevada Regional Professional Development Program
North Las Vegas, NV

Sharlene E. Ricks
Alpine School District
American Fork, UT

Debbie Rutherford
Independent National Consultant
Omaha, NE

Melinda Springli
Lawton Public Schools
Lawton, OK

Kerry Stephenson
Pendleton County School District
Butler, KY

Photography: Cover © Ingeborg Knol/Panther Media/age fotostock; Interior models, Tom Dubanowich; p. 3 © Bill Ross/Corbis; p. 105 © Michael T. Sedam/Corbis; p. 207 © Veer; p. 309 © Visions of America/Joe Sohm/Getty Images

Art Credits: pp. 4, 30, 56, 106, 158, 208, 160, 310, 336 Mike Dammer; pp. 17, 28, 54 Dave Aikin; pp. 95, 132, 234, 362, 365, 387 Chris Vallo

ISBN 978-0-7367-7277-8

Zaner-Bloser, Inc.
1-800-421-3018
www.zaner-bloser.com
Printed in the United States of America 11 12 13 14 15 19840 5 4 3 2 1

Hi, there! We're your *Strategies for Writers* Writing Partners!

We're here to guide you step-by-step through the stages of the writing process: Prewrite, Draft, Revise, Edit, and Publish.

In each unit, we'll focus on one mode of writing: **narrative, informative/explanatory, opinion,** or **descriptive**.

Have you ever wondered how to write a fable? Or what the elements of a how-to paper are? How about some reasons for writing an opinion speech or a descriptive paper? We'll answer those questions and more.

We'll focus on these six traits of effective writing: **Ideas, Organization, Voice, Word Choice, Sentence Fluency,** and **Conventions**. We'll explain how to apply the traits to each genre of writing, and we'll show you how the traits work together.

In each chapter, we'll first review a model writing sample. Then we'll use a rubric to score the model. Rubrics are a great way to know exactly what is expected as you plan and evaluate your writing. After that, it's your turn to write!

Narrative writing

Table of Contents

Informative/Explanatory writing

Table of Contents

Opinion writing

Table of Contents

Descriptive writing

Table of Contents

Appendices

Appendix A: Grammar Practice

Table of Contents

Narrative writing tells a story.

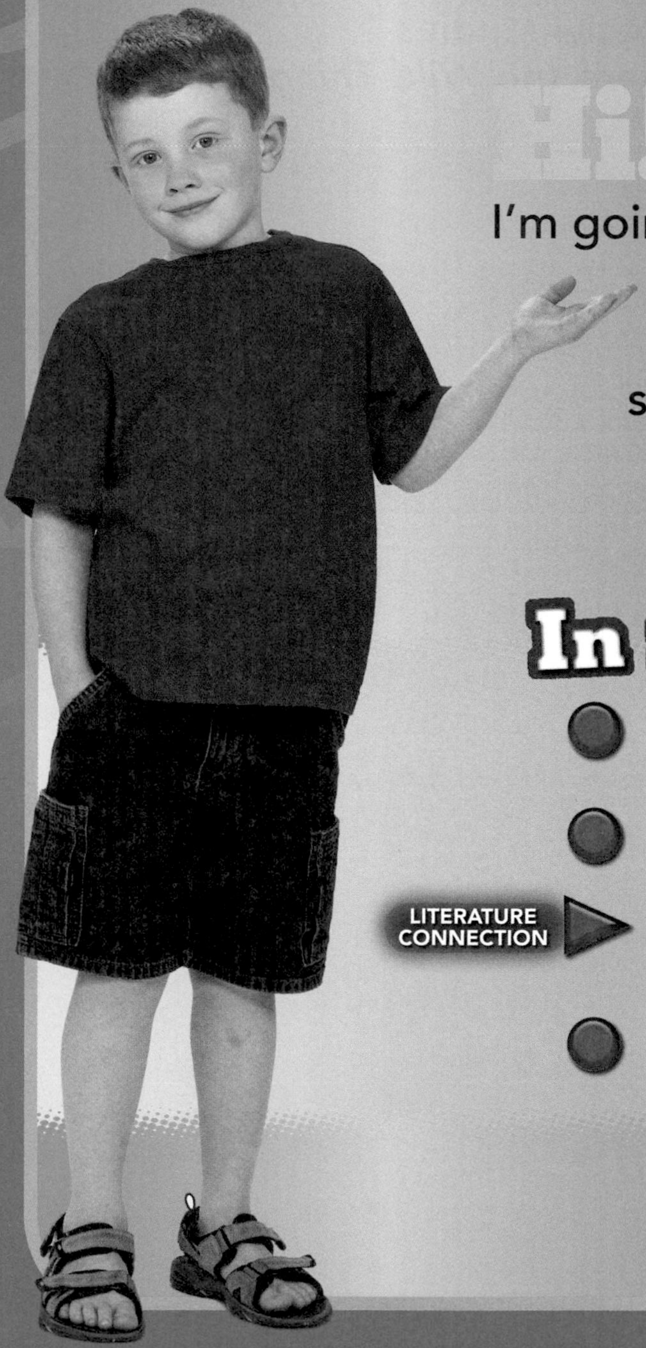

Hi! I'm Kyle. I live in Oregon, and I'm a writer like you. I'm going to learn how to write narratives. I'll start with a story about me. Read on to see how I do it.

In this unit

- Personal Narrative
- Friendly Letter
- LITERATURE CONNECTION ▶ Fable
- Writing for a Test

Name: Kyle
Home: Oregon
Hobbies: swimming, playing checkers
Favorite Subject: social studies
Favorite Book: *Where the Wild Things Are* by Maurice Sendak
Favorite Food: spaghetti

Parts of a Personal Narrative

A personal narrative tells about an event from my life. It could be something that I did or something that happened to me.

Narrator
A narrator is the person who tells the story. In a story about me, I am the narrator.

Setting
This is where and when the story takes place. It could be this morning on the bus or last month at a park.

Plot
This is what happens in the story. I might tell about one event or many events.

Structure
A story about me should have a beginning, a middle, and an ending.

Character(s)
Characters are the people in my story. In a story about me, I might be the only character. My friends, classmates, and family could be characters, too.

Reasons for Writing a Personal Narrative

Here are some reasons to write a personal narrative.

To entertain
When something interesting happens, I want to tell people about it. My story might be funny, surprising, or exciting.

To remember
Sometimes things happen that I want to remember. Writing a story helps me do that. It also helps me think about what the event meant to me.

To tell information
When I find out important information, I want to pass it on. If I visit someplace special or try to do something new, I can tell other people about it in a story.

Linking Narrative Writing Traits to a Personal Narrative

In this chapter, you will write a story about an experience you had. This is called a personal narrative. Kyle will guide you through the stages of the writing process. He will also show you some writing strategies that are linked to the Narrative Writing Traits below.

Narrative Writing Traits

Ideas	• a clear topic or plot • details that describe actions, thoughts, or feelings
Organization	• the events in order • a strong beginning and ending • transitions that show the order of events
Voice	• a voice that speaks directly to the audience • if used, dialogue that fits the characters
Word Choice	• exact words that tell the story
Sentence Fluency	• sentences that are smooth
Conventions	• no or few errors in spelling, punctuation, and capitalization

Let's look at this model of a personal narrative. Michele wrote a story about learning to ride her bike. After reading her story, we can use the rubric on the next two pages to check her writing.

Personal Narrative MODEL

setting

characters

structure

narrator

plot

The Day I Learned to Ride a Bike
by Michele Cho

On Saturday, my dad took me out on my new bike. First, I pedaled. Dad ran behind me and held my bike seat. We did that over and over. Next, Dad let go. I didn't know he wasn't holding on. I just kept riding down the street. All of a sudden, the bike felt different. Then I knew I was riding all by myself. I felt like a race car driver. Dad said he was very proud of me. The last thing I did that day was ride around the block by myself.

Personal Narrative Rubric

	6	5	4
Ideas	The topic is clear. Details describe actions, thoughts, and feelings well.	The topic is clear. Most details describe actions, thoughts, or feelings.	The topic is somewhat clear. Some details describe actions, thoughts, or feelings.
Organization	The events are in order. Time-order words show the order of events.	Most of the events are in order. Some time-order words are used.	The order of events is confusing. More time-order words are needed for the order to be clear.
Voice	The writer's personality comes through strongly in the writing.	The writer's personality comes through in the writing.	The writer's personality comes through most of the time.
Word Choice	The words used are exact and create a strong picture of the writer.	The words used create a strong picture of the writer.	Most of the words help the reader picture the writer.
Sentence Fluency	Sentences of different lengths make the story easy and fun to read.	Most of the sentences are varied and the piece is easy to read.	Some sentences are varied in length. The writing is a little bit choppy.
Conventions	All sentences are capitalized and punctuated correctly.	The meaning is clear, even with one or two errors in capitalization and punctuation.	A few errors in capitalization and punctuation do not interfere with meaning.

+Presentation Use neat handwriting or word processing.

What makes a good personal narrative? A rubric can help you decide. Use it to help you write. Then use it again to check your writing.

	3	2	1
Ideas	The topic is clear only in parts of the story. The story needs more details.	The topic is not clear. The details do not describe anything well.	The topic is not clear. There are not enough details.
Organization	The events may not be in order. Time-order words are not used correctly.	The events are not in order. The writing is hard to follow.	Understanding the writing is difficult because the writing lacks any organization.
Voice	The writer's personality comes through occasionally but is not consistent.	The writer's personality is inconsistent or lacking in the piece.	The writer's personality is missing in the piece.
Word Choice	Some of the words help the reader form a picture of the writer.	Words used are wrong. They do not create a clear picture of the writer.	The words do not help the reader picture the writer.
Sentence Fluency	Many sentences are the same length and make the story choppy to read.	Sentences are usually the same length, and the reader must work to read the piece.	Sentences are too long, lack variety, or are incomplete. The writing is hard to follow.
Conventions	Some errors in capitalization and punctuation can confuse the reader.	Many errors stop the reader and interfere with understanding.	Serious, frequent errors make the writing hard to read.

See Appendix B for 4-, 5-, and 6-point narrative rubrics.

Using the Personal Narrative Rubric to Study the Model

Let's use the rubric to check Michele's story about how she learned to ride her bike.

Ideas

- The topic is clear.
- Details describe actions, thoughts, and feelings well.

I think Michele's topic is interesting. Many kids learn to ride a bike. It feels great! Michele explains the feeling really well.

> All of a sudden, the bike felt different. Then I knew I was riding all by myself.

Organization

- The events are in order.
- Time-order words show the order of events.

Michele starts at the beginning and tells each event that happened until the end of her story. All of the events in the story are in the right order. The word *first* shows the order of events.

First, I pedaled. Dad ran behind me and held my bike seat. We did that over and over.

Voice

- The writer's personality comes through strongly in the writing.

Words like *I* and *me* make it sound as if Michele is talking right to the reader. Saying how she feels helps her personality come through in her writing.

I felt like a race car driver.

Word Choice

- The words used are exact and create a strong picture of the writer.

Michele said that she felt like a race car driver. That gives me a good idea of how she felt! She chose words that help me "see" how she was feeling.

> I felt like a race car driver.

Sentence Fluency

- Sentences of different lengths make the story easy and fun to read.

There are many sentences of different lengths in Michele's story. Some are short and some are long. This makes her story flow.

> Dad said he was very proud of me. The last thing I did that day was ride around the block by myself.

Conventions

- All sentences are capitalized and punctuated correctly.

I read the story again and found that every telling sentence is capitalized and ends with a period. Here's an example.

I just kept riding down the street.

Presentation Use neat handwriting or word processing.

My Turn!

Now it's my turn. I'm going to write my own story. Keep reading to see how I will do it.

Prewrite

Focus on **Ideas**

The Rubric Says The topic is clear.

Writing Strategy Make a list of interesting topics and pick the best one.

Before writing my own story I need to pick a topic. The rubric says that my topic should be clear, which means that I also have to have details that tell about the topic. First, I will make a list of topics. Next, I'll write some notes about each one. The notes will help me to pick the best topic. I'll circle my choice. After that, I'll write my own personal narrative.

Writer's Term

Topic

A **topic** is the idea you choose to write about.

My Topics	My Notes
the day my mom came home from the army	That was a great day, but a lot happened. It's too much for one story.
my first day of day camp	That was last summer. That's too long ago.
my first swimming lesson	Some of my friends are taking swimming lessons now. Others have already learned how to swim. This topic would interest all of my friends. I'll use it!

Reflect

Read Kyle's notes. Do you agree that it made sense to choose this topic?

Apply

Make a list of topics you could write about. Write some notes next to each topic. Choose the best topic.

Prewrite

Focus on **Organization**

The Rubric Says The events are in order.

Writing Strategy Make a Storyboard to organize the events.

Now I need to organize the events in my story. That means I need to tell what happened first, then, next, and last. The rubric says that the events in my story should be in order. I will make a Storyboard to help me organize my story.

Writer's Term

Storyboard

A **Storyboard** uses pictures to show what happens in a story. The pictures show the events in order.

Topic: My First Swimming Lesson

Reflect

Does the Storyboard help you imagine what happened first, next, and last in Kyle's story?

Apply

Now you try! Make your own Storyboard. Use this page as a model.

Draft

Focus on **Ideas**

The Rubric Says Details describe actions, thoughts, and feelings well.

Writing Strategy Use details to describe actions, thoughts, and feelings.

Next I will use my Storyboard to write a draft. I'll write sentences to tell what happened. I'll be sure to use details to tell the reader what is happening and how I am feeling. Interesting details will keep the reader's attention.

Writer's Term

Details

Details tell about the topic. A detail can tell what is happening or how someone is feeling.

Proofreading Marks

- / Make a small letter
- ∧ Add something
- ℓ Take out something
- ⊙ Add a period
- ≡ Make a capital letter

[DRAFT]

details

Do you like to swim. My first swimming lesson was hard I was afraid of the water. we had to learn to float my teacher was Ms. Lindsay She said she would help by holding me up in the water. she put her hands on my waist. I put my head back in the water. I put my feet up. we did that lots of times. Ms. Lindsay asked me to try it without her. I did it. I floated all by myself. Everyone clapped.

Reflect

Kyle used details about how he felt and what happened. Did they make the story interesting?

Apply

Now you try it. Look at your topic notes and your Storyboard. Write your first draft with details.

Revise

Focus on **Ideas**

The Rubric Says Details describe actions, thoughts, and feelings well.

Writing Strategy Add details about thoughts and feelings.

I will read my draft to check my writing. I know that I need to include plenty of details. Details will help readers understand my story. I've done a good job describing what happened, but I think I should add more details that explain my thoughts and feelings.

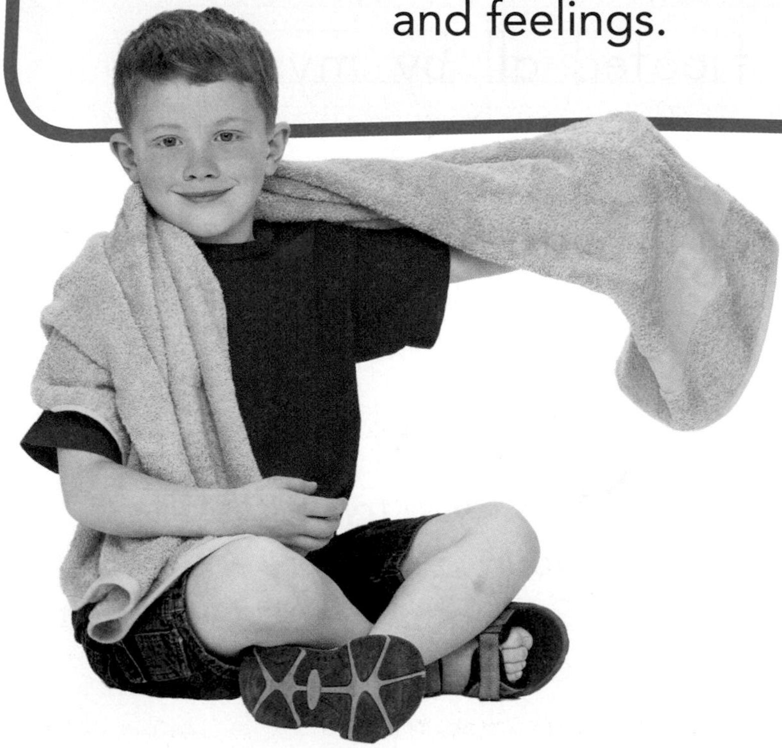

[DRAFT]

Do you like to swim. My first swimming lesson was hard I was afraid of the water. we had to learn to float I wouldn't even try it. my teacher was Ms. Lindsay. She was really nice to me. She said she would help by holding me up in the water. she put her hands on my waist. I put my head back in the water. I put my feet up. we did that lots of times. Ms. Lindsay asked me to try it without her.

added details

Reflect

Look at what Kyle added. Do the details give you a better idea of what he thought and felt?

Apply

Now look at your draft. Make sure you have included plenty of details.

Revise

Focus on Organization

The Rubric Says Time-order words show the order of events.

Writing Strategy Use words like *first, then, next,* and *finally* to show the order of events.

I will read my draft to check my writing. I know that every event should be told in order. Before I wrote my story, I looked at my Storyboard. It showed me when things happened. I will add some time-order words, like *first, then,* and *next,* to help the reader follow my story.

Writer's Term

Time-order Words

Time-order words show the order of events in a story. Examples of time-order words are **first, next, then, last,** and **finally**.

[DRAFT]

was afraid of the water. we had to
learn to float. I wouldn't even
try it. my teacher was Ms. Lindsay
She was really nice to me. She said
she would help by holding me up in
the water. First, she put her hands on
my waist. Then, I put my head back
in the water. Next, I put my feet up.
we did that lots of times. Ms. Lindsay
asked me to try it without her. Finally,
I did it. I floated all by myself.
Everyone clapped.

added time-order words

Reflect

Kyle added time-order words. Do they help you follow the story?

Apply

Now look at your draft. Check the order of the events. Make sure you use time-order words.

Edit

Focus on **Conventions**

The Rubric Says All sentences are capitalized and punctuated correctly.

Writing Strategy Capitalize the first word of each sentence and put punctuation at the end of each sentence.

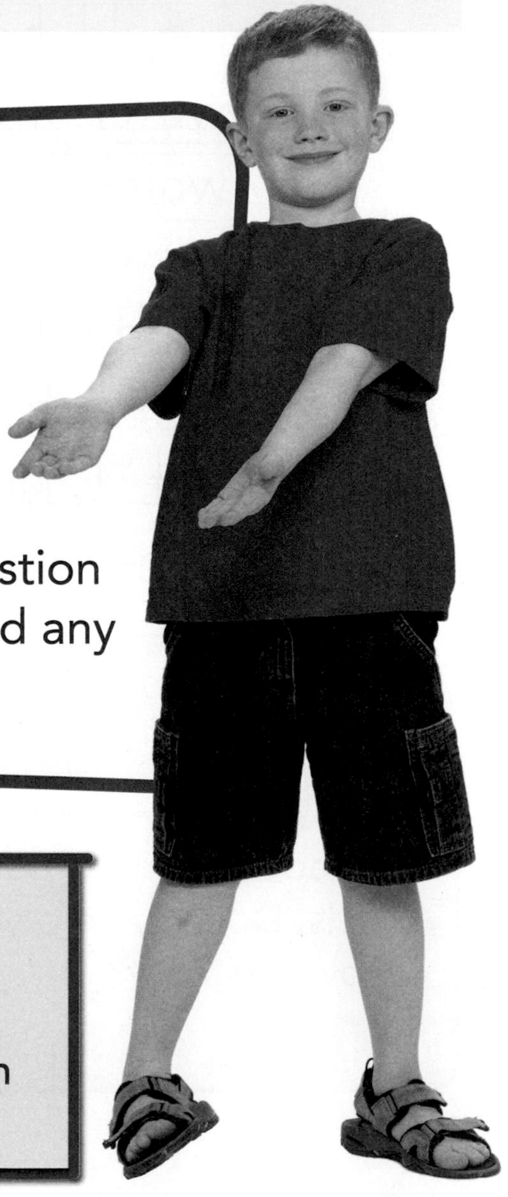

Now I need to edit my story. That means I'll fix the mistakes. I will check to make sure every sentence starts with a capital letter. My telling sentences need to end with a period. My asking sentences need to end with a question mark. I'll proofread my story to find any sentences that I need to fix.

Writer's Term

Telling and Asking Sentences

A **telling sentence** gives information. It ends with a period. An **asking sentence** asks a question. It ends with a question mark.

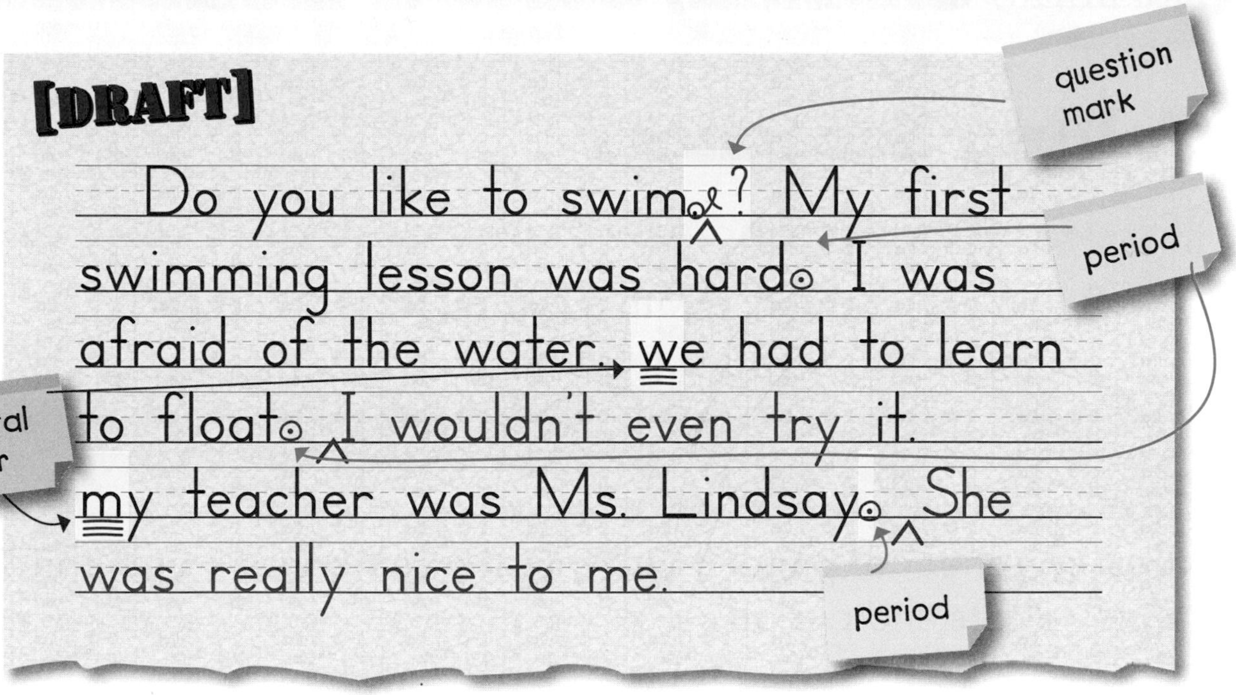

[DRAFT]
Do you like to swim? My first
swimming lesson was hard I was
afraid of the water. we had to learn
to float I wouldn't even try it.
my teacher was Ms. Lindsay She
was really nice to me.
question mark
period
capital letter
period

Reflect

Look at Kyle's edits. Did he capitalize the beginning of each sentence? Did he use periods and question marks correctly?

Apply

For more practice writing sentences correctly, turn to the next page.

Telling Sentences

Know the Rule

Begin each sentence with a **capital letter**. End each telling sentence with a **period**.

Practice the Rule

Number a sheet of paper 1–8. Write the sentences. Put in the capital letters and periods.

1. he jumps in the pool
2. i get in slowly
3. now I am all wet
4. my brother splashes me
5. now I splash my brother
6. the water is cold
7. the line for the diving board is long
8. a playground is next to the pool

Asking Sentences

Know the Rule

Begin each sentence with a **capital letter**. End each asking sentence with a **question mark**.

Practice the Rule

Number a sheet of paper 1–8. Write the sentences. Put in the capital letters and question marks.

1. when will we get to the beach
2. can we go swimming right away
3. do you want to go in the water right now
4. what is that crawling on the sand
5. is that a crab
6. will it pinch me
7. is the towel covered with sand
8. is it time to go home yet

Publish

+Presentation

Publishing Strategy	Put the story in a class album.
Presentation Strategy	Use neat handwriting or word processing.

I plan to put my story in the class album. Before I do that, I will make a neat final copy. The checklist below will help me make sure my story is ready to be published. You can use the checklist with your story, too.

My Final Checklist

Did I —

- ✔ use my best handwriting or word processing?
- ✔ check my spelling?
- ✔ capitalize and punctuate sentences correctly?

FINAL DRAFT

My First Swimming Lesson

by Kyle

Do you like to swim? My first swimming lesson was hard. I was afraid of the water. We had to learn to float, but I wouldn't even try it. My teacher was Ms. Lindsay. She was really nice to me. She said she would help by holding me up in the water. First, she put her hands around my waist. Then, I put my head back in the water. Next, I put my feet up. We did that lots of times. Ms. Lindsay asked me to try it without her. Finally, I did it. I floated all by myself, and everyone clapped. I felt so proud of myself! I couldn't wait until my next lesson.

Apply

Now it's time to publish your story. Use the rubric to check your final draft.

Parts of a Friendly Letter

A friendly letter is a letter I write to a friend or a family member. It can be about something I did or about something that happened. It has five parts.

Heading
The heading is at the top of the page. It shows the writer's address and the date of the letter.

Greeting
The greeting names the reader. It begins with *Dear* and ends with a comma.

Body
The body of the letter tells the reader the message.

Closing
The closing is at the end of the letter. It might say *Your friend* or *Sincerely*. It ends with a comma.

Signature
The writer signs his or her name below the closing.

Reasons for Writing a Friendly Letter

Here are some reasons to write a friendly letter.

To share stories
I like to tell my friends and family about interesting things I've done. They like to hear about what I've been doing.

To keep in touch
I like to keep in touch with people I don't see very often. Even though they are far away, we can stay close by writing letters.

To do something nice
A personal letter shows that you care. It takes time and thought to write a letter.

Linking Narrative Writing Traits to a Friendly Letter

In this chapter, you will write a letter to a friend or family member. This is called a friendly letter. Kyle will guide you through the stages of the writing process. He will also show you some writing strategies that are linked to the Narrative Writing Traits below.

Narrative Writing Traits

Ideas	• a clear topic or plot • details that describe actions, thoughts, or feelings
Organization	• the events in order • a strong beginning and an ending • transitions that show the order of events
Voice	• a voice that speaks directly to the audience • if used, dialogue that fits the characters
Word Choice	• exact words that tell the story
Sentence Fluency	• sentences that are smooth
Conventions	• no or few errors in spelling, punctuation, and capitalization

Let's look at this model of a friendly letter. Charlie tells his grandma about a class field trip to a dairy. We can use the rubric on the next page to check his letter.

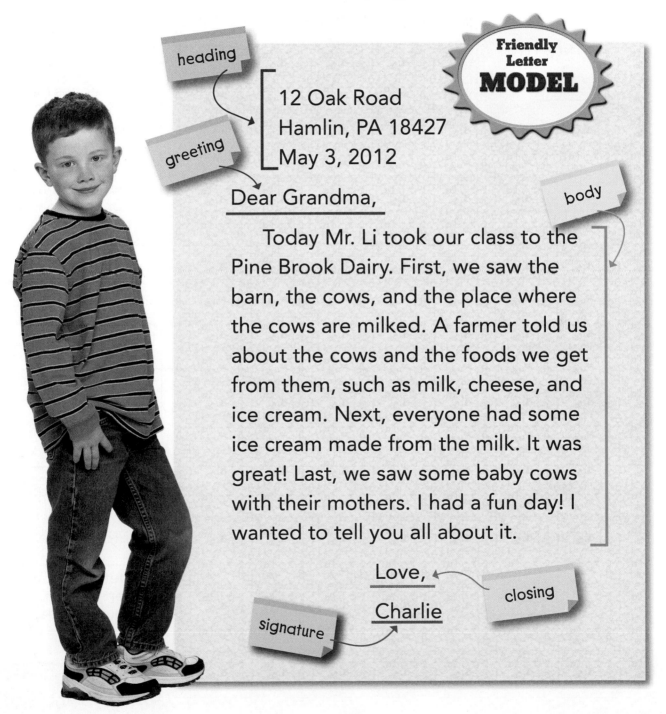

Friendly Letter MODEL

heading

12 Oak Road
Hamlin, PA 18427
May 3, 2012

greeting

Dear Grandma,

body

Today Mr. Li took our class to the Pine Brook Dairy. First, we saw the barn, the cows, and the place where the cows are milked. A farmer told us about the cows and the foods we get from them, such as milk, cheese, and ice cream. Next, everyone had some ice cream made from the milk. It was great! Last, we saw some baby cows with their mothers. I had a fun day! I wanted to tell you all about it.

Love, — closing

Charlie — signature

Friendly Letter Rubric

	6	5	4
Ideas	The letter has a main topic. Interesting details describe the topic.	The letter has a main topic. Most of the details are interesting.	The letter has more than one topic. Some of the details are confusing.
Organization	The letter is organized in five parts. Time-order words show the order of events.	The letter is almost organized. Time-order words show the order of most events.	The letter is missing one or more parts. Some time-order words are incorrect.
Voice	The writer's voice is natural and polite.	The writer's voice usually sounds natural and polite.	The writer's voice sounds natural and polite most of the time.
Word Choice	The words used are clear and exact.	Many words are clear and exact.	One or two more exact words are needed.
Sentence Fluency	Sentences of different lengths make the letter easy and fun to read.	Most of the sentences are varied and the piece is easy to read.	Some sentences are the same length. The writing is choppy.
Conventions	The letter has all five parts. Commas are correct in the date and address.	The letter has all five parts. Most commas are correct in the date and address.	The letter has a few errors, but the meaning is clear.

+Presentation The letter is neat and has all five parts.

What makes a good friendly letter? A rubric can help you decide. Use it to help you write. Then use it again to check your writing.

3	2	1	
The letter has more than one topic with few details.	The topic of the letter is unclear. Details are missing or unrelated.	The writing does not have a topic. Sentences are unrelated and random.	Ideas
The letter is missing several parts. More or better time-order words are needed.	The writing is not organized like a letter. No time-order words are used.	The writing is a collection of random thoughts with no organization.	Organization
The writer's voice sounds natural and polite some of the time.	The writer's voice sounds far away some of the time.	The writer's voice sounds awkward or flat.	Voice
Some of the words are too general.	Many words are repeated. Some are used incorrectly.	The words chosen are confusing, vague, or misused.	Word Choice
Many sentences are the same length and make the letter choppy to read.	Sentences are usually the same length. The reader must work to read the piece.	Sentences are too long, lack variety, or are incomplete. The writing is hard to follow.	Sentence Fluency
Some errors confuse the reader.	Many errors stop the reader. The reader must reread to understand.	Serious, frequent errors make the letter hard to read and understand.	Conventions

See Appendix B for 4-, 5-, and 6-point narrative rubrics.

Using the Friendly Letter Rubric to Study the Model

Let's use the rubric to check Charlie's letter about his visit to a dairy.

Ideas

- The letter has a main topic.
- Interesting details describe the topic.

Charlie wrote his main topic in the very first sentence of his letter. I know that the rest of his letter probably will be about what he saw and did at the dairy.

Today Mr. Li took our class to the Pine Brook Dairy.

Organization

- The letter is organized in five parts.
- Time-order words show the order of events.

The letter tells what happened at the beginning, the middle, and the end of the visit to the dairy. Here is an event from the beginning of the story.

> First, we saw the barn, the cows, and the place where the cows are milked.

Voice

- The writer's voice is natural and polite.

Charlie's letter is friendly and sounds just like a boy talking to his grandmother about a trip. His last sentences show that he is excited to share his story with his grandmother.

> Next, everyone had some ice cream made from the milk. It was great! Last, we saw some baby cows with their mothers. I had a fun day! I wanted to tell you all about it.

Word Choice • The words used are clear and exact.

I read a lot of interesting details in the letter. I like how Charlie tells exactly what kinds of foods come from cows.

A farmer told us about the cows and the foods we get from them, such as milk, cheese, and ice cream.

Sentence Fluency • Sentences of different lengths make the letter easy and fun to read.

Charlie uses short and long sentences. Different kinds of sentences make his letter flow.

Next, everyone had some ice cream made from the milk. It was great!

Conventions

- The letter has all five parts.
- Commas are correct in the date and address.

Charlie's letter has a heading, a greeting, a body, a closing, and a signature. They are all written correctly. Here are his closing and signature.

Love,
Charlie

Presentation The letter is neat and has all five parts.

My Turn!

Now it's my turn. I'm going to write my own friendly letter. Read on to see how I will do it.

Prewrite

Focus on **Ideas**

The Rubric Says The letter has a main topic.

Writing Strategy Pick a topic that has interesting details.

Before writing my own friendly letter to my friend Jade, I need to pick a topic. The rubric says my letter needs a main topic. I will think about what I would like to tell Jade. Then I'll make a list of topics and write some details about each one. These notes will help me pick the best topic. After that, I'll write my own friendly letter.

Writer's Term

Topic

A **topic** is the idea you choose to write about. It is what the letter is all about.

My Topics	My Notes
my trip to Ohio	A lot happened on that trip. We were gone two weeks. There's too much to tell.
what I did yesterday	I just stayed home yesterday. Not much happened. That's not a very interesting topic.
my babysitter's wedding	That was fun! Jade probably never went to a wedding like that. There are plenty of interesting details I can tell her about. I'll write about that!

Reflect

Think about a topic that has plenty of interesting details. What would you like to write to a friend about?

Apply

Make a list of topics. Write some notes next to each one. Then choose the best topic.

Prewrite

Focus on **Organization**

The Rubric Says The letter is organized in five parts.

Writing Strategy Use a Web to organize the events in the body.

The rubric says that my letter should have five parts: heading, greeting, body, closing, and signature. The body is the most important. That is where I will tell Jade all the details about my babysitter's wedding. I'll make a Web so I don't forget any of the details for the body.

Writer's Term

Web

A **Web** shows details or events from a story. The topic goes in the center box. The details go in the outside boxes.

Graphic Organizer: Web

bride and groom started under huppah

groom broke a glass

Topic

My Babysitter's Wedding

bride and groom lifted on chairs

everyone ate and danced

Reflect

Look at the events in Kyle's Web. Which one should he write about first?

Apply

Make a Web for the details that will be in the body of your letter. Which detail will you write about first? Which detail will be next?

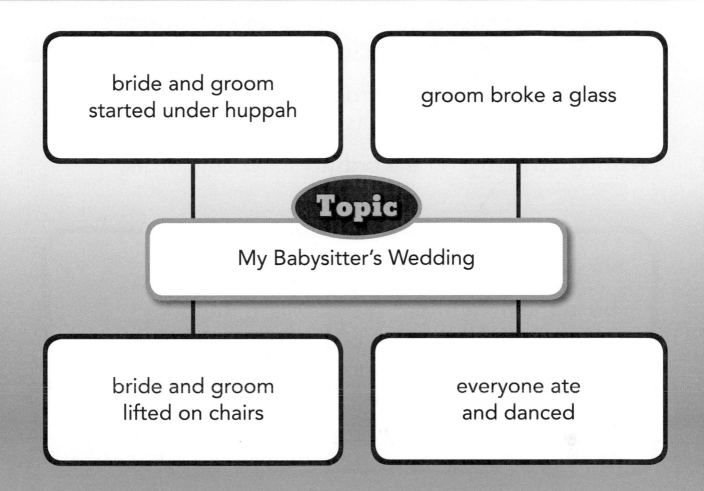

Draft

Focus on **Organization**

The Rubric Says Time-order words show the order of events.

Writing Strategy Use words to show time order.

A friendly letter has five parts that have to be in the right order. The details in the body of my letter have to be in the right order, too. Otherwise, my letter won't make any sense! I'll use some time-order words to help Jade know what happened first, next, and last.

Writer's Term

Time-order Words

Time-order words are words that show the order of events. Words like **first, next, then, last,** and **finally** are time-order words.

Proofreading Marks

- / Make a small letter
- ∧ Add something
- Take out something
- ⊙ Add a period
- ≡ Make a capital letter

[DRAFT]

Oct. 27 2012

Dear Jade,

Last week, I went to my babysitter's wedding. First, the bride and groom stood under a tent. Next, there was a big party. Everyone danced in a circle. We had a big meal. We had more dancing.

heading · greeting · body · time-order words

Reflect

Look at the draft of Kyle's letter. Does the order of events make sense? Does he use any time-order words?

Apply

Now you try it. Look at your topic notes and your Web. Write your first draft.

Revise

Focus on **Voice**

The Rubric Says The writer's voice is natural and polite.

Writing Strategy Write as if you are talking to a friend.

Next I'll read my draft to check my writing. The rubric says that my voice needs to be natural. That means that my letter should sound polite. But I also want to sound like I am just talking to a friend. I'll add some informal words.

Writer's Term

Natural

Writing that is **natural** sounds the way that people really talk. It is friendly and personal.

[DRAFT]

Dear Jade,

Last week, I went to my babysitter's wedding. It was so much fun! First, the bride and groom stood under a tent. Next, there was a big party. Everyone danced in a circle. We had a big meal. We had more dancing.

added informal words

Reflect

Kyle added a sentence. Does it help make his writing sound like he is talking to a friend?

Apply

Look at the draft of your friendly letter. Can you add some words to make your writing sound more natural?

Revise

Focus on **Word Choice**

The Rubric Says The words used are clear and exact.

Writing Strategy Use exact words.

The rubric says the words should be clear and exact. Exact words help readers "see" what I am describing in my letter. If my words are too general, they won't describe what I am talking about. After rereading my draft, I see a place where I can use exact words. They will help explain a word that some readers might not know.

[DRAFT]

added exact words

First, the bride and groom stood under a tent called a huppah. A huppah is a special, pretty canopy with open sides and a flat roof. Next, there was a big party. We had a big meal. We had more dancing.

Reflect

Kyle added exact words. Do they help you understand the writing better?

Apply

Now look at your draft. Make sure you use exact words.

Edit

Focus on Conventions

The Rubric Says The letter has all five parts. Commas are correct in the date and address.

Writing Strategy Check for all parts of a letter and the commas.

Next I will proofread my letter. I'll check that I've included all five parts of a friendly letter. If I forgot a part, I will add it where it belongs. I'll also make sure the commas in the date and address are correct.

[DRAFT]

added the rest of the heading

19 North Street
Sherwood, OR 97140
Oct. 27, 2012

added comma

Dear Jade,

Last week, I went to my babysitter's wedding. It was so much fun! First, the bride and groom stood under a tent called a huppah. A huppah is a special, pretty canopy with open sides and a flat roof.

Reflect

Kyle added a comma to the date. Is the comma in the address correct?

Apply

Check your draft. Make sure you include all five parts of a friendly letter. Are your commas correct? Turn to the next page for more practice with the parts of a letter and commas.

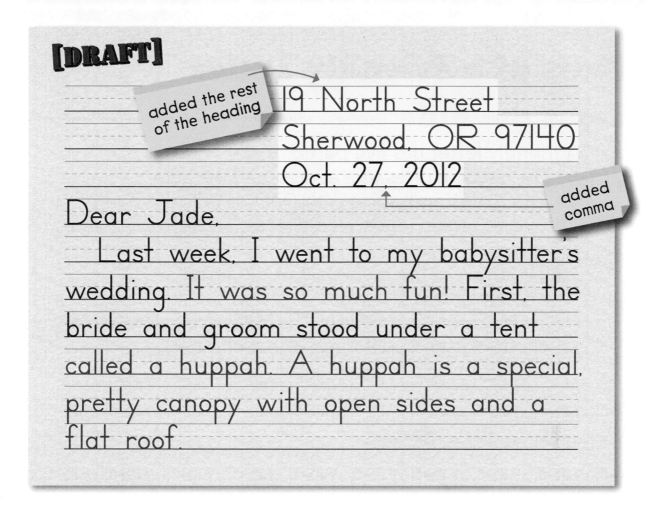

Parts of a Friendly Letter

Know the Rule

A friendly letter has five parts.

- The **heading** gives your address and the date.
- The **greeting** begins with *Dear*. It tells the name of the person you are writing to, and it ends with a comma.
- The **body** is the main part of the letter.
- The **closing** is one word or more, such as *Love, Your pal,* or *Your cousin*. The closing begins with a capital letter, and it ends with a comma.
- The **signature** is your name.

Practice the Rule

Number a sheet of paper 1–5. Write the part of a friendly letter described by each sentence.

1. This is where you write your name at the end of a letter.
2. This part begins with the word *Dear*.
3. This part includes your address and the date.
4. This is the main message of your letter.
5. This part is where you say goodbye.

Commas in Dates and Addresses

Know the Rule

In an **address** a comma is used between the name of the city and the name of the state. In a **date** a comma is used after the day of the month but before the year.

Practice the Rule

Number a sheet of paper 1–8. Write each address or date with the commas in the correct places.

1. 3 Maple Street Lincoln ME 04457
2. 300 Oceanview Avenue San Francisco CA 94108
3. 52 Main Street Elwood NE 68937
4. 20 South Alfred Road Troy OH 45373
5. October 24 2013
6. December 3 2014
7. June 21 2012
8. February 11 2013

Publish

+Presentation

Publishing Strategy Mail the letter.

Presentation Strategy Make sure the letter is neat.

I finished editing my letter! I'll make a neat final copy. First, I will use this checklist to make sure I've finished everything. You can use this list to check your final draft, too. Then, I'll write Jade's address on an envelope, add a stamp, and mail her the letter.

My Final Checklist

Did I —

✔ check my spelling?

✔ include all five parts of a friendly letter?

✔ use commas correctly in the address and date?

✔ write neatly?

FINAL DRAFT

19 North Street
Sherwood, OR 97140
Oct. 27, 2012

Dear Jade,

Last week, I went to my babysitter's wedding. It was so much fun! First, the bride and groom stood under a tent called a huppah. A huppah is a special, pretty canopy with open sides and a flat roof. Then, the groom broke a glass with his foot. Next, there was a big party. Everyone danced in a circle. People lifted up the bride and groom on chairs. Finally, we had a big meal and more dancing.

Your friend,
Kyle

Reflect

How did Kyle do? Did he follow the rubric correctly? Be sure to use the rubric to check your own final draft.

Parts of a Fable

Do you know the fable about a lion and a mouse? The lion saves the mouse's life. The mouse promises to help the lion. The big lion laughs, but one day the tiny mouse helps the lion! The lesson is that even someone tiny can help someone big and strong.

A fable is a story that teaches a lesson. Sometimes, the last sentence of the fable explains the lesson.

Character(s)
The characters in a fable are often animals that talk and act like people.

Problem
One of the characters has a problem to solve.

Solution
The characters find a solution to the problem.

Lesson
Fables have a lesson for the reader to learn.

Plot
That's what happens in the fable.

Reasons for Writing a Fable

Here are some reasons to write a fable.

To entertain
Fables are fun to read. A fable usually tells a story that everyone can understand and enjoy.

To teach a lesson
A fable can show people how to treat each other. Reading about how a character solves a problem can help you solve the same kind of problem.

To share culture
Many cultures have fables that have been told again and again, even for hundreds of years! I can write a fable that tells something about my own culture, too.

Linking Narrative Writing Traits to a Fable

In this chapter, you will write a story that teaches a lesson. This is called a fable. Kyle will guide you through the stages of the writing process. He will also show you some writing strategies that are linked to the Narrative Writing Traits below.

Narrative Writing Traits

Ideas	• a clear topic or plot • details that describe actions, thoughts, or feelings
Organization	• the events in order • a strong beginning and ending • transitions that show the order of events
Voice	• a voice that speaks directly to the audience • if used, dialogue that fits the characters
Word Choice	• exact words that tell the story
Sentence Fluency	• sentences that are smooth
Conventions	• no or few errors in spelling, punctuation, and capitalization

Let's look at this model of a fable. It's a lot like the fable about the lion and the mouse. We can use the rubric to check Chad's fable.

Fable MODEL

Lily and the Firefighter

by Chad Haziz

One day, little Lily was playing with a ball. The ball got stuck on Ms. Ramos's roof.

Ms. Ramos said, "Don't worry, Lily. I'll get the ball for you."

Ms. Ramos got her the ball.

Lily said, "I will help you one day, Ms. Ramos."

Ms. Ramos laughed. How could a small, quiet girl like Lily help her? Ms. Ramos was a brave, strong firefighter.

A month later, an empty house on Lily's street was on fire. Lily knew what to do! She ran to Ms. Ramos. Lily told her there was a puppy in that house. Ms. Ramos went straight to the house. She saved the puppy! Quiet little Lily turned out to be a big help after all.

plot

characters

problem

solution

lesson

Fable Rubric

	6	5	4
Ideas	The plot and characters are clear and interesting.	The plot and characters are clear.	Some plot events are not clear.
Organization	The beginning, middle, and end are in order and complete.	The beginning, middle, and end are mostly in order and complete.	Some events are out of order. The ending is somewhat complete.
Voice	The dialogue makes the characters act and talk like unique, real people.	Most of the dialogue makes the characters act and talk like real people.	Usually the characters talk like real people. Their personalities are recognizable.
Word Choice	Well-chosen adjectives make the writing very clear.	Adjectives are used in an appropriate way.	Most adjectives are used appropriately.
Sentence Fluency	Sentences of different lengths make the story easy and fun to read.	Most of the sentences are varied and the piece is easy to read.	Some sentences are the same length. The writing is choppy.
Conventions	Adjectives are well chosen. Quotation marks are used correctly.	Adjectives are well chosen. There are one or two errors with quotation marks.	Adjectives are used. Some errors with quotation marks confuse the reader.

+Presentation Use good spacing between words and lines.

What makes a good fable? A rubric can help you decide. Use it to help you write. Then use it again to check your writing.

	3	2	1
Ideas	The plot is not clear. Some details about the characters are confusing.	The story lacks a plot. The characters are not developed.	The writer's ideas are not clear.
Organization	Many events are out of order. The ending leaves the reader with questions.	Events are out of order. The writing doesn't have an ending.	The writing is hard to understand because it is not organized.
Voice	Some of the characters sound the same. It is hard to tell who is speaking.	Only the narrator speaks. The characters do not talk.	There is no recognizable voice in the piece with the characters or the narrator.
Word Choice	Only very general adjectives are used. They do not make the writing clear.	Some adjectives are wrong for the writing.	No adjectives are used.
Sentence Fluency	Many sentences are the same length and make the story choppy to read.	Sentences are usually the same length. The reader must work to read the piece.	Sentences are too long, lack variety, or are incomplete. The writing is hard to follow.
Conventions	Better adjectives are needed. Many errors with quotation marks confuse the reader.	No adjectives are used. Errors with quotations make the writing hard to understand.	Many serious errors make the writing very hard to understand.

See Appendix B for 4-, 5-, and 6-point narrative rubrics.

Using the Fable Rubric to Study the Model

Let's use the rubric to check Chad's fable about Lily and the firefighter.

Ideas

- The plot and characters are clear and interesting.

This fable is interesting! It sounds a lot like "The Lion and the Mouse." A quiet little girl helps a strong, grown-up firefighter, just like the tiny mouse helps the big, strong lion. The end of Chad's fable tells the same lesson as the famous fable.

> Quiet little Lily turned out to be a big help after all.

Organization

- The beginning, middle, and end are in order and complete.

The fable has a beginning, middle, and end. Here's the beginning. It introduces the two main characters, Lily and Ms. Ramos.

> One day, little Lily was playing with a ball. The ball got stuck on Ms. Ramos's roof.

Voice

- The dialogue makes the characters act and talk like unique, real people.

Chad has his characters talk like real people. The dialogue between Lily and Ms. Ramos sounds just like two people having an ordinary conversation.

> Ms. Ramos said, "Don't worry, Lily. I'll get the ball for you."

Word Choice

- Well-chosen adjectives make the writing very clear.

Chad's fable has lots of describing words that tell about the characters. Look at this sentence. It uses two adjectives to make Ms. Ramos more real. Can you find them?

> Ms. Ramos was a brave, strong firefighter.

Sentence Fluency

- Sentences of different lengths make the story easy and fun to read.

Chad uses different kinds of sentences in his fable. Here is a long sentence followed by a short one. Mixing long and short sentences keeps readers interested!

> A month later, an empty house on Lily's street was on fire. Lily knew what to do!

Conventions

- Adjectives are well chosen.
- Quotation marks are used correctly.

Quotation marks go at the beginning and at the end of what someone says. In this sentence, the words that Lily says are in quotation marks.

Lily said, "I will help you one day, Ms. Ramos."

Presentation Use good spacing between words and lines.

My Turn!

Now it's my turn. I'm going to write my own fable. Keep reading to see how I will do it.

Prewrite

Focus on Ideas

The Rubric Says The plot and characters are clear and interesting.

Writing Strategy Pick a fable readers will like. Make notes about how to rewrite it.

Now I need to pick a fable to rewrite. My favorite fable is "The Grasshopper and the Ant." The ant works all summer to save food for winter. The grasshopper sings and plays. When winter comes, the ant has food, but the grasshopper has none. The lesson is to plan ahead if you want something. I'm going to rewrite this fable. I'll change the animals to people. I'll make the story happen now! First I need to prewrite, or plan, my story. To do that, I'll make notes about my fable.

My Fable

Jen and Jule

- want to go to the water park
- parents will take them if they earn money

My Notes

Jen	Jule
• like the ant • saves allowance • does special jobs for pay • has money for water park	• like the grasshopper • spends allowance • doesn't do anything extra • has no money for water park

Lesson—Plan ahead if you want something.

Reflect

Did Kyle do what the rubric said? Will his notes help him rewrite the fable in his own way?

Apply

Make a list of ideas for your fable. Write notes about the plot and characters.

Prewrite

Focus on **Organization**

The Rubric Says The beginning, middle, and end are in order and complete.

Writing Strategy Make a Story Map to tell what happens at the beginning, middle, and end of the fable.

After I write my notes, I'll organize the events in my fable. I will make a Story Map to help organize my ideas! The rubric says I need to make sure my fable has a complete beginning, middle, and end. I'll put my notes in order on my Story Map.

Writer's Term

Story Map

A **Story Map** tells the events of a story in the order that they happen.

My Fable: Jen and Jule

Beginning

Problem—Jen and Jule need money for water park

Middle

Jen—saves money
does special jobs for pay

Jule—spends money
doesn't do anything extra

End

Jen—has money to go

Jule—has no money to go

Lesson—Plan ahead if you want something.

Reflect

Did Kyle include all of the important events of his fable? Are the events in order?

Apply

Make notes for your fable. Then organize your fable by making your own Story Map.

Draft

Focus on **Voice**

The Rubric Says The dialogue makes the characters act and talk like unique, real people.

Writing Strategy Write dialogue for the story.

The rubric says my characters should sound like real people when they talk. So as I am writing, I need to do two things. First, I need to tell a story that has a lesson. Second, I need to have the characters talk for themselves. Readers need to be able to hear the voices of my characters, not just me as a writer. And each character has to sound different.

Writer's Term

Dialogue

Dialogue is what the characters in a story say to each other.

[DRAFT]

Proofreading Marks

- / Make a small letter
- ∧ Add something
- ℓ Take out something
- ⊙ Add a period
- ≡ Make a capital letter

Jen and Jule wanted to go to Water World.

Their parents said, If you can pay to get in, we will take you.

Every week, Jen saved money. She did special jobs for pay. Jule spent all her money on snacks. She was going to sell lemonade. She never did it. At the end of the month, Jen had money for Water World.

dialogue

Reflect

How did Kyle do? What parts of a fable has he written so far? Did he include dialogue?

Apply

Now you try it. Look at your notes and your Story Map. Start writing your first draft.

Revise

Focus on Word Choice

The Rubric Says Well-chosen adjectives make the writing very clear.

Writing Strategy Add words that describe the characters.

Next, I'll read my fable to revise my writing. The rubric says that I should use well-chosen adjectives. Adjectives tell about my characters and make them more real for my reader! I'll use sticky notes to add describing words for my characters.

Writer's Term

Adjectives

Adjectives are words that describe people, places, or things. **Little, strong, quiet,** and **brave** are examples of adjectives.

[DRAFT]

added adjectives

Every week, smart Jen saved money. She did special jobs for pay. Silly Jule spent all her money on snacks. She was going to sell lemonade. She never did it. At the end of the month, Jen had money for Water World.

Reflect

Do the adjectives Kyle added change what you think about his characters?

Apply

Now look at your draft. Add adjectives to make your characters more real.

Revise

Focus on Sentence Fluency

The Rubric Says Sentences of different lengths make the story easy and fun to read.

Writing Strategy Vary the lengths of the sentences.

I need to reread my draft to make sure I have both short sentences and long sentences. Sentences that are all about the same length can sound boring and choppy. I will count the number of words in each sentence. If there are too many long sentences, I will make some shorter. If there are too many short sentences, I will make them longer or combine some.

[DRAFT]

combined sentences

Silly Jule spent all her money on snacks. She was going to sell lemonade, but She never did it. At the end of the month, Jen had money for Water World.

Reflect

Look at Kyle's revisions. Do the changes make his fable more interesting to read?

Apply

Count the number of words in each sentence of your fable. Make sure you have a mix of short sentences and long sentences.

Edit

Focus on Conventions

The Rubric Says Adjectives are well chosen. Quotation marks are used correctly.

Writing Strategy Check the adjectives and quotation marks.

Next, I'll check my spelling and punctuation to make sure there are no mistakes. I'll see if I can add any more adjectives to better describe my characters. I will also check to see if I used quotation marks correctly.

Writer's Term

Quotation marks

Quotation marks (" ") show where a person's spoken words begin and end. "A mouse can sometimes help a lion," the mouse said.

[DRAFT]

added quotation marks

Their parents said, "If you can pay to get in, we will take you."

Every week, smart Jen saved money. She did special jobs for pay. Silly Jule spent all her money on snacks. She was going to sell lemonade~~.~~, but ~~S~~she never did ~~it~~. At the end of the month, happy Jen had money for Water World.

"I'm ready to go!" she said.

added adjective

Reflect

Kyle added quotation marks. Is his draft easier to read now? He also added an adjective. Does it describe Jen better?

Apply

Check your draft to make sure you used quotation marks correctly. Can you add another adjective?

Adjectives

Know the Rule

An **adjective** is a word that describes a person, place, or thing. *Pretty, noisy,* and *brave* are examples of adjectives.

Example: A brave firefighter saved the puppy.

Practice the Rule

Number a sheet of paper 1–6. Write the adjectives in each sentence on your paper.

1. A strange dog crossed the street by my house.
2. My little brother began to cry.
3. Our next-door neighbor, Tom, said, "Why are you crying, Kevin?"
4. Kevin was sure that the dog was a mean dog.
5. "I think I will get a bad bite from the dog," said Kevin.
6. Tom is a brave police officer. He told us never to touch a dog we don't know.

Quotation Marks

Know the Rule

Use quotation marks to show where speech begins and ends. After a quote, place a comma or end punctuation inside the quotation marks: "I will help you someday," said the mouse.

Practice the Rule

Number a sheet of paper 1–8. Write the sentences. Add quotation marks to show where each person's speech begins and ends.

1. Did you hear that Mark broke his arm? asked Lisa.
2. What happened? said Tonya.
3. Lisa said, He crashed his bike.
4. That's terrible! Tonya said.
5. Should we go visit him? asked Lisa.
6. That's a good idea, said Tonya.
7. When should we go? asked Lisa.
8. Tonya said, Let's go now!

Publish

+Presentation

Publishing Strategy Read the fable to the class.

Presentation Strategy Use good spacing between words and lines.

I finished my fable! I'll read it aloud to my class. Our teacher said we might record our fables, too! If I leave spaces between the words and the lines, my fable will be easier to read. Of course, I will remember to speak clearly and with good expression! Here's a checklist I will use to publish my fable.

My Final Checklist

Did I —

✔ use adjectives well?

✔ use quotation marks correctly?

✔ use good spacing?

FINAL DRAFT

Jen and Jule

by Kyle

Jen and Jule wanted to go to Water World.

Their parents said, "If you can pay to get in, we will take you."

Every week, smart Jen saved money. She did special jobs for pay. Silly Jule spent all her money on snacks. She was going to sell lemonade, but she never did. At the end of the month, happy Jen had money for Water World.

"I'm ready to go!" she said.

Sad Jule had nothing but empty snack boxes. If you need money, you have to plan ahead, work hard, and save!

Reflect

Did Kyle follow the rubric? Be sure to use the rubric to check your own final draft.

Narrative test writing

Read the Writing Prompt

Every writing test starts with a writing prompt. Most writing prompts have three parts:

Setup This tells what you need to know to get ready for writing.

Task This tells exactly what you're supposed to write.

Scoring Guide This part tells how your writing will be scored. To do well on the test, you should include everything on the list.

A scoring guide is a lot like a rubric. It lists everything you need to think about to write a good paper. Many scoring guides will have the same parts as the rubrics we've looked at:

- Ideas
- Organization
- Voice
- Word Choice
- Sentence Fluency
- Conventions

Writing MODEL Prompt

Have you ever done something for the first time? Were you excited? Were you scared? Think about one of these times.

Write a personal narrative about something you did for the very first time.

Be sure your personal narrative

- has a clear topic and descriptive details.
- uses time-order words to show the order of events.
- uses a writer's voice that sounds natural.
- has exact words.
- has short and long sentences.
- has correct capitalization, punctuation, and spelling.

Writing Traits in the Scoring Guide

The scoring guide on page 83 has been made into this chart. How is it like the rubrics you've been using? Not all test prompts have all six writing traits. This one does!

Ideas	• Be sure your narrative has a clear topic and descriptive details.
Organization	• Be sure your narrative uses time-order words to show the order of events.
Voice	• Be sure your narrative uses a writer's voice that sounds natural.
Word Choice	• Be sure your narrative has exact words.
Sentence Fluency	• Be sure your narrative has short and long sentences.
Conventions	• Be sure your narrative has correct capitalization, punctuation, and spelling.

Look at Tory Perez's story. Did she follow the scoring guide?

My First Sleepover

Writing Prompt **MODEL** Response

by Tory Perez

My next-door neighbor is also my best friend. I was so happy when Ann asked me to stay at her house overnight! It would be my first sleepover!

First, I packed my toothbrush. Then, I packed my pajamas. Last, I packed a pillow and sleeping bag. I was ready!

I was excited, but I was scared, too. I might miss my mom. What if I wanted to go home?

I had so much fun! We had pizza for supper. We played checkers. We watched a movie and ate popcorn. Then I called my mom to say goodnight. We turned off the lights and talked and giggled. For breakfast we had blueberry pancakes. Ann is coming to my house for a sleepover next week!

Using the Scoring Guide to Study the Model

Now let's use the scoring guide to check Tory's writing test, "My First Sleepover."

Ideas

- The narrative has a clear topic and descriptive details.

Tory's topic is very interesting. I can't wait to go on my first sleepover! Tory gives lots of details about what a sleepover is like. She tells about what she packed, ate, and did on the sleepover.

I had so much fun! We had pizza for supper. We played checkers. We watched a movie and ate popcorn.

Organization

- The narrative uses time-order words to show the order of events.

Tory uses the words *first, then,* and *last* to describe getting ready for her sleepover.

First, I packed my toothbrush. Then, I packed my pajamas. Last, I packed a pillow and sleeping bag. I was ready.

Voice

- The narrative has a voice that sounds natural.

Tory uses the words *I* and *me*. That makes it sound like Tory is talking right to the reader. I can tell how excited she is because she says how she feels in the first few sentences.

My next-door neighbor is also my best friend. I was so happy when Ann asked me to stay at her house overnight! It would be my first sleepover!

Using the Scoring Guide to Study the Model

Word Choice • The narrative uses exact words.

Tory uses exact words to tell readers that she is happy about the sleepover. But she is nervous, too.

> I was excited, but I was scared, too. I might miss my mom. What if I wanted to go home?

Sentence Fluency • The narrative has short and long sentences.

Tory uses different kinds of sentences. Some are long and some are short. This keeps her narrative interesting—and it helps me want to keep reading!

> We played checkers. We watched a movie and ate popcorn. Then, I called my mom to say goodnight.

Conventions

- The narrative has correct capitalization, punctuation, and spelling.

Be sure to look for any mistakes that you make often. Tory did not make any mistakes at all in capitalization or punctuation. Her final draft doesn't have any errors.

Many tests are timed. Your teacher will tell you how much time you have to take a test. Look on the next two pages for some tips on how to plan your time and take a test.

Planning My Time

Look at the picture of the clock. Do you see that there is more green than any other color? That means I should spend most of my time getting ready to write. What takes the least amount of time?

Remember these important tips when you write for a test.

TEST TIPS

1. **Study the writing prompt before you start to write.**
2. **Make sure you understand the task before you start to write.**
3. **Keep an eye on the clock.**
4. **Reread your writing. Compare it to the scoring guide at least twice.**
5. **Plan, plan, plan!**
6. **Write neatly.**

Prewrite

Focus on **Ideas**

Writing Strategy Study the writing prompt and choose a topic.

Getting ready to write is very important. First, I will read the prompt so that I know what to do. See how I circled the important words? These words tell me exactly what I will write. I need to write a story about something special I did with a friend or a relative.

Then, I need to pick a topic. I plan to write about a trip I took with my Grand Pop. We went fishing! I'll also need to write some notes about it.

Finally, I will use the scoring guide on page 83. It will guide me as I write, revise, and edit.

My Writing Test Prompt

Setup — Have you ever done something special with a friend or relative? Was it something you did for the very first time? Did something surprising happen? Think about one of these times.

Task — Write a personal narrative about something special you did with a friend or a relative.

Here are my notes about my fishing trip with my grandfather.

Notes

- I went fishing with Grand Pop.
- We drove to the middle of the pond in his boat.
- We forgot the fishing poles.
- We forgot the worms.
- We bought fish at a store on the way home.

Apply

Before writing, think about a time you could tell about. Pick a topic that has enough details. Then write some notes.

Prewrite

Focus on Organization

Writing Strategy Make a graphic organizer.

I have some notes. Now I need to put them in order. A Storyboard will help me. A Storyboard uses pictures to show what happens in a story. The pictures show the events in order. A Storyboard will help me remember all the parts of my story.

Topic: My Fishing Trip With Grand Pop

Reflect

Look at Kyle's Storyboard. How will it help him to remember everything that happened? Are the events in order?

Apply

Make your own Storyboard. Look at your notes. Draw a picture of each event. Make sure they are in order.

Draft

Focus on Ideas

Writing Strategy Use clear details to describe the event.

The first thing I need to do is write my main topic. I'll put it in my first sentence. That way, my readers will know what my narrative will be about. The details about my topic will come next.

I'll follow my Storyboard to make sure I get all the details. It will also help me put the events in order.

As I write, I will check the scoring guide. That will help keep me on track. If I stay on track, I should do well on my test.

Proofreading Marks

- / Make a small letter
- ∧ Add something
- Take out something
- ⊙ Add a period
- ≡ Make a capital letter

[DRAFT]

The Funny Fishing Trip

Grand Pop invited me to go fishing with him.

We drove to the middle of the pond in Grand Pop's motorboat. We realized that we forgot the fishing poles! We forgot the worms! Back to the dock we went. We started to fish.

We laughed and laughed about our funny fishing trip. we stopped at a store on our way home and bout some fish Grand Pop promised to take me fishing again soon.

Reflect

Read the draft. What is the topic? Are there enough details?

Apply

Write your own draft. Be sure the topic is clear. Include plenty of details.

Revise

Focus on **Ideas**

Writing Strategy Add details to make the topic clear.

The scoring guide says that my topic needs to be clear. I'll read the writing task again. It says to write about something special I did with a friend or a relative.

I think my topic sentence needs more work. I will add a detail about Grand Pop. I will also tell why the fishing trip was special.

[DRAFT]

added details to make topic clear

The Funny Fishing Trip

Grand Pop, my grandfather, invited me to go fishing with him. It was my first time fishing!

We drove to the middle of the pond in Grand Pop's motorboat. We realized that we forgot the fishing poles! We forgot the worms! Back to the dock we went. We started to fish.

We laughed and laughed about our funny fishing trip. we stopped at a store on our way home and bout some fish Grand Pop promised to take me fishing again soon.

Reflect

Is Kyle's topic clear? Are there plenty of details?

Apply

Reread the scoring guide. Make sure your narrative has a clear topic and descriptive details.

Revise

Focus on Organization

Writing Strategy Use words such as *first, then, next, last*, and *finally* to show the order of events.

I will reread my draft. I might be able to make my story better. My middle paragraphs are kind of confusing. There is a lot going on. The scoring guide says I should use time-order words. Words such as *first, then, next, last*, and *finally* tell when things happen. I will add some of these words to help the reader follow my story.

[DRAFT]

First, ~~W~~e drove to the middle of the pond in Grand Pop's motorboat. Then, ~~W~~e realized that we forgot the fishing poles! We forgot the worms! Back to the dock we went. Finally, ~~W~~e started to fish.

We laughed and laughed about our funny fishing trip. we stopped at a store on our way home and bout some fish Grand Pop promised to take me fishing again soon.

added time-order words

Reflect

Look at Kyle's revisions. He added time-order words. Do they help you follow the story?

Apply

Look at your draft. Did you tell your story in order? Make sure you add some time-order words, such as *first, then, next, last*, and *finally*.

Edit

Focus on Conventions

Writing Strategy Check the capitalization, punctuation, and spelling.

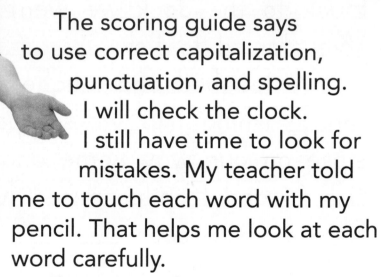

The scoring guide says to use correct capitalization, punctuation, and spelling. I will check the clock. I still have time to look for mistakes. My teacher told me to touch each word with my pencil. That helps me look at each word carefully.

There are a few mistakes in my last paragraph. I need to mark my corrections neatly. On a test there is no chance to make a final copy.

FINAL DRAFT

The Funny Fishing Trip
by Kyle

Grand Pop, my grandfather, invited me to go fishing with him. It was my first time fishing!

First, We drove to the middle of ~~the pond~~ Maxwell Pond in Grand Pop's motorboat. Then, We realized that we forgot the fishing poles! ~~We forgot~~ and the worms! Back to the dock we went. Finally, We started to fish.

We laughed and laughed about our funny fishing trip. we stopped at a ~~store~~ fish market on our way home and ~~bout~~ bought some fish. Grand Pop promised to take me fishing again soon. That would be great!

Reflect

What do you think of Kyle's story?

Informative/ Explanatory writing

gives information.

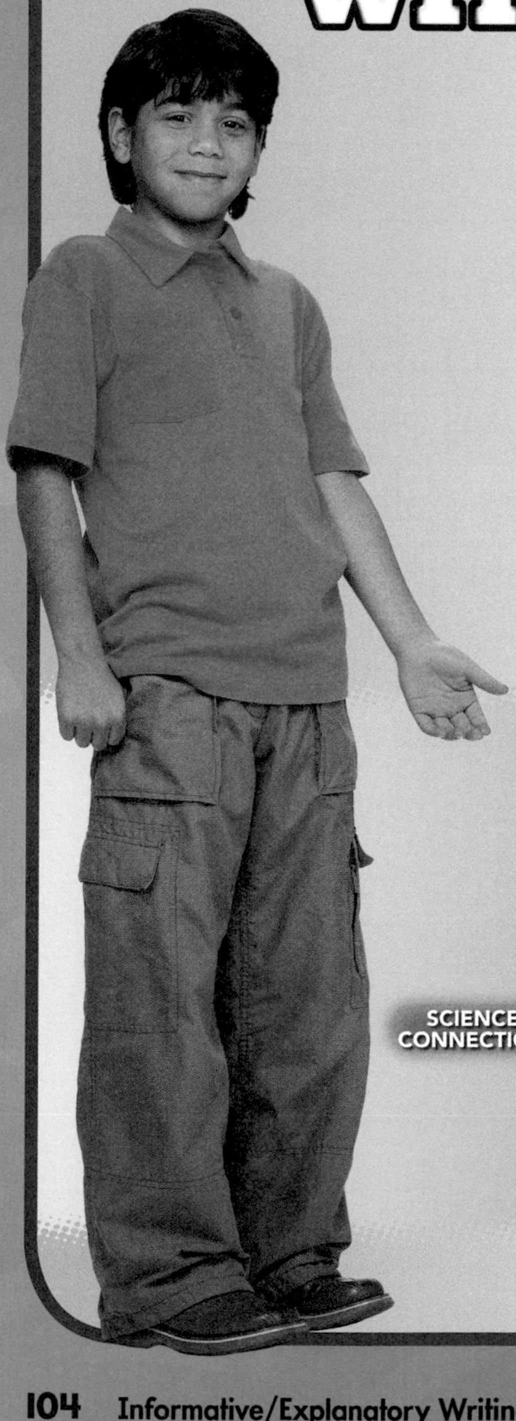

Hi! My name is Max. I live in New Mexico. I'm going to write a how-to paper. A how-to paper explains how to do or make something. Read on to see how I will do it.

In this unit

- How-To Paper
- Compare-and-Contrast Paper
- SCIENCE CONNECTION ▶ Research Report
- Writing for a Test

Name: Max
Home: New Mexico
Hobbies: basketball, word games
Favorite Subject: science
Favorite Book: *The Magic School Bus Inside a Hurricane* by Joanna Cole
Favorite Food: buñuelos

Parts of a How-To Paper

A how-to paper tells about the steps in a process. It can tell how to make something or how to do something.

Topic
The topic is what my paper is about. I will tell the reader how to do or make something.

Steps
I will tell how to do or make something in steps. I'll tell one part at a time so the reader can understand what I mean.

Introduction
The introduction is at the beginning of my paper. It tells what my topic is.

Body
The body is the middle of the paper. This is where I write the steps of how to do or make something.

Conclusion
The conclusion is the end of my paper. I try to sum up my paper in this part.

Reasons for Writing a How-To Paper

Here are some reasons to write a how-to paper.

To tell information
When I want to explain how to do something, I can write instructions that make it easy to understand. Maybe my friend wants to know how I make my special peanut butter-banana sandwiches. I can tell him exactly how I do it in a how-to paper.

To give reasons
Sometimes I need to explain what I've done. For example, I can write a how-to paper for my science class. I can tell step-by-step how I did an experiment, and why I did it that way.

To record observations
I could watch my brother do something, such as take care of a puppy. Then I can write a how-to paper about it. That way, I will know how to do it myself the next time!

Linking Informative/Explanatory Writing Traits to a How-To Paper

In this chapter, you will write a how-to paper. Max will guide you through the stages of the writing process. He will also show you some writing strategies that are linked to the Informative/Explanatory Writing Traits below.

Informative/Explanatory Writing Traits

Ideas	• a clear, focused topic • accurate and complete supporting details
Organization	• a strong introduction, body, and conclusion • facts that develop the topic • transitions that connect ideas
Voice	• a voice that connects directly to the reader
Word Choice	• exact words
Sentence Fluency	• different types of sentences for variety
Conventions	• no or few errors in spelling, punctuation, and capitalization

Let's look at this model of a how-to paper. Leo tells how to make a piñata. We can use the rubric on the next two pages to check his writing.

How-To Paper MODEL

introduction

topic

body

steps

conclusion

How To Make a Piñata

by Leo Trader

Any party can be great if you have a piñata. I'll tell you how you can make a piñata. Get a balloon and a newspaper. You will also need flour, water, paint, and scissors. First, blow up the balloon and tie it. Then, cut the newspaper into small strips. Next, mix the flour and water to make glue. Dip the paper strips in the glue and cover the balloon with them. Put two layers of newspaper on the balloon. Let the piñata dry. You can paint the piñata after it's dry. Cut a flap in the bottom. Take out the balloon. Finally, fill your piñata with candy and tape the flap closed. You're ready for a party!

How-To Paper Rubric

	6	5	4
Ideas	The topic is clear and detailed. The steps of the process are perfectly outlined.	The topic is interesting. The steps in the process are clear.	The topic is interesting. One or two steps are not clear.
Organization	The organization and time-order words perfectly describe the order of the steps.	All of the steps are in the right order. Time-order words connect the steps.	Most of the steps are in the right order. One or two time-order words are needed.
Voice	The writer speaks directly to the reader with confidence.	The writer speaks directly to the reader.	The writer speaks directly to the reader most of the time.
Word Choice	The writing uses active, strong verbs. The words are carefully chosen.	Strong verbs explain what to do.	Some verbs could be more exact.
Sentence Fluency	Sentences are easy to follow because they begin in varied and helpful ways.	All sentences are easy to follow.	Most of the sentences are easy to follow.
Conventions	Sentences are clear and punctuation is correct. Prepositions are used correctly.	A few errors with punctuation and prepositions can be easily corrected.	Some errors with punctuation and prepositions confuse the reader.

+Presentation The paper uses only one or two readable fonts.

What makes a good how-to paper? A rubric can help you decide. Use it to help you write. Then use it again to check your writing.

3	2	1	
The topic is interesting. Many of the steps are not clear.	The topic is not clear. The steps may not belong together.	The process is not addressed in a way the reader can follow at all.	Ideas
The steps may be out of order. Time-order words may be confusing.	The steps are not in any order. The reader has trouble following the steps.	The piece has no logical order and the reader is confused.	Organization
The writer speaks to the reader only in the beginning.	The writer does not speak directly to the reader.	The writing lacks voice. The writer is not present.	Voice
Some verbs are used incorrectly.	Many verbs are used incorrectly or are weak and not active.	Words chosen do not explain a process.	Word Choice
Many sentences are difficult to follow.	Some sentences begin the same way. The reader could be confused.	Many sentences are incomplete.	Sentence Fluency
Many errors with punctuation and prepositions make the reader struggle to understand.	Many errors with punctuation and prepositions leave the reader confused.	The paper has not been edited.	Conventions

See Appendix B for 4-, 5-, and 6-point Informative/Explanatory rubrics.

Using the How-To Paper Rubric to Study the Model

Let's use the rubric to check Leo's how-to paper about how to make a piñata.

Ideas

- The topic is clear and detailed. The steps of the process are perfectly outlined.

The topic is clear from Leo's topic sentence. In the rest of his paper, Leo outlines the steps for how to make a piñata.

> I'll tell you how you can make a piñata.

Organization

- The organization and time-order words perfectly describe the order of the steps.

The steps that Leo wrote about make sense. They are easy to follow. He used the time-order words *First, Then, Next,* and *Finally* to describe the order of the steps. Here's the last step. *Finally* tells the reader that this is the last step.

> Finally, fill your piñata with candy and tape the flap closed.

Voice

- The writer speaks directly to the reader with confidence.

All through his paper, Leo used the word *you*. He spoke right to the reader. His opening sentence is an example of speaking directly to the reader with confidence.

> Any party can be great if you have a piñata.

Word Choice

- The writing uses active, strong verbs. The words are carefully chosen.

Leo was very precise in his choice of verbs. They tell you exactly what to do. They are simple to follow. Verbs like *blow, cut, mix, dip, paint,* and *fill* are very clear and strong. Here's an example of how Leo used active, strong verbs:

> Dip the paper strips in the glue and cover the balloon with them.

Sentence Fluency

- Sentences are easy to follow because they begin in varied and helpful ways.

Leo began his sentences in different ways and gave helpful information. Here's an example:

> Let the piñata dry. You can paint the piñata after it's dry.

Conventions

- Sentences are clear and punctuation is correct.

All of the punctuation is correct. The last sentence ends with an exclamation point to show Leo's excitement.

You're ready for a party!

+Presentation The paper uses only one or two readable fonts.

My Turn!

Now it's my turn. I'm going to write my own how-to paper. Keep reading to see how I will do it.

Prewrite

Focus on **Ideas**

The Rubric Says The topic is clear and detailed.

Writing Strategy Think about what you know how to do. Pick a topic that your reader will enjoy learning about.

My topic has to have enough details to be interesting. But the topic can't have too many details. That will confuse the readers. I'll make a list of things I know how to do. Then I'll write ideas about each topic and decide which one is most interesting. I'll use that topic to write my how-to paper.

My Topics	My Notes
• how to build a snowman	• That's nothing new to anyone. We can all do that. It wouldn't be an interesting topic.
• how to build a model airplane	• That's interesting, but it's too hard. It would take too long to explain.
• how to make a jigsaw puzzle	• This topic is perfect! I think my classmates would be interested in it. I know a great way to make a jigsaw puzzle. I'll use this topic.

Reflect

Do you think Max's topic will be interesting to read about?

Apply

Make a list of topics that you know about. Write notes about each topic. Pick the best topic.

Prewrite

Organization

The Rubric Says	The organization and time-order words perfectly describe the order of the steps.
Writing Strategy	Make an Order Chain to organize the events.

Next I need to organize the steps in my how-to paper. The rubric says the how-to steps should be in the right order. I'll make an Order Chain that tells each step in making a jigsaw puzzle.

Writer's Term

Order Chain

An **Order Chain** shows the steps of a how-to paper in order, from first to last.

Graphic Organizer: Order Chain

Topic: How To Make a Jigsaw Puzzle

First Step	Find an interesting picture from a magazine and cut it out.
Next Step	Cut a piece of heavy paper the same size as the picture.
Next Step	Paste the picture on the heavy paper.
Next Step	Wait for the paste to dry. Draw two wavy lines across and two wavy lines down the back of the paper.
Last Step	Cut the picture apart on the lines.

Reflect

Do Max's steps make sense? Did he include all of the important information?

Apply

Write your notes in an Order Chain.

Draft

Focus on Ideas

The Rubric Says The steps of the process are perfectly outlined.

Writing Strategy Introduce the topic clearly and include all the steps.

Next I'll use my Order Chain to write a draft. If my readers want to make their own jigsaw puzzles, they will need to know every step. I'll put the topic at the beginning of the introduction. Then I'll make sure that I tell about every step.

Proofreading Marks

- / Make a small letter
- ∧ Add something
- ℓ Take out something
- ⊙ Add a period
- ≡ Make a capital letter

[DRAFT]

Have you ever made a puzzle I have This is how to do it. Find a colorful picture in a magazine. Pictures of the outdoors work best. Cut a piece of paper so it's the same size as the picture. Put the picture on the heavy paper. Let the paste dry. Draw two wavy lines across the back of the paper. Draw two wavy lines down the back of the paper. Cut the picture apart in the lines. Now you have the pieces of a puzzle.

Reflect

Read Max's draft. Are the steps clear?

Apply

Now you try it. Look at your topic and your Order Chain. Write your first draft.

Revise

Focus on Ideas

The Rubric Says The steps of the process are perfectly outlined.

Writing Strategy Make sure the steps are complete.

Now it's time to revise my draft to make it even better. The rubric says that the steps have to be very clear. I'll read my draft to see where I can add information. My readers will not be able to follow my directions if I leave out any information.

[DRAFT]

added information

Have you ever made a jigsaw puzzle I have This is how to do it. Find a colorful picture in a magazine. Pictures of the outdoors work best. Cut a piece of heavy paper so it's the same size as the picture. Put the picture on the heavy paper. Let the paste dry. Draw two wavy lines across the back of the paper. Draw two wavy lines down the back of the paper. Cut the picture apart in the lines. Now you have the pieces of a puzzle.

Reflect

Did Max include all the steps to make a jigsaw puzzle?

Apply

Read through the steps. Are they all there? Are they complete?

Revise

Focus on **Organization**

The Rubric Says The organization and time-order words perfectly describe the order of the steps.

Writing Strategy Use time-order words to show the order of the steps.

I will read my paper again to make sure I'm following the rubric. It says I need to use time-order words to show the order of the steps. Time-order words help readers know when to do each step. I'll read my draft to see where I can add some time-order words to make my writing more clear.

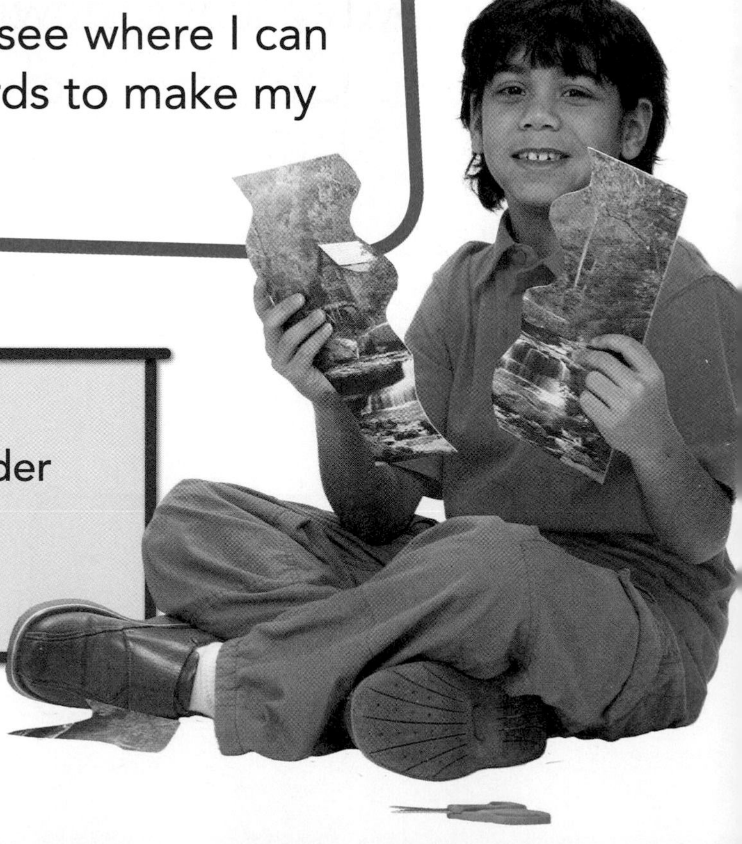

Writer's Term

Time-Order Words

Time-order words tell the order things happen. Examples of time-order words are *first, next, soon.*

[DRAFT]

Have you ever made a jigsaw puzzle I have This is how to do it. First, find a colorful picture in a magazine. Pictures of the outdoors work best. Then, cut a piece of heavy paper so it's the same size as the picture. Next, put the picture on the heavy paper. Let the paste dry. Draw two wavy lines across the back of the paper. Draw two wavy lines down the back of the paper. Finally, cut the picture apart in the lines. Now you have the pieces of a puzzle.

added time-order word

added time-order words

added time-order word

Reflect

Max added some time-order words. Do you think the steps are clearer now?

Apply

Now look at your draft. Add time-order words to show the order of steps in your paper.

Edit

Focus on Conventions

The Rubric Says Sentences are clear and punctuation is correct. Prepositions are used correctly.

Writing Strategy Make sure that prepositions and punctuation are correct.

Next I will edit my paper. I always proofread my writing to look for problems with spelling and sentences. I'll make sure that I've used periods, question marks, and exclamation points correctly. I'll also check to be sure I used the right prepositions.

Writer's Term

Prepositional Phrases

A **prepositional phrase** helps tell where something is. It begins with a preposition and ends with a noun. Examples of prepositional phrases are **on the table, in the library,** and **by the tree**.

[DRAFT]

added question mark

added period

Have you ever made a jigsaw puzzle? I have. ~~This is~~ I'll tell you how to do it. First, ~~F~~find a colorful picture in a magazine. Pictures of the outdoors work best. Then, ~~C~~cut a piece of heavy paper so it's the same size as the picture. Next, ~~Put~~ paste the picture on the heavy paper. Let the paste dry. Draw two wavy lines across ~~the back of the paper. Draw~~ and two wavy lines down the back of the paper. Finally, ~~C~~cut the picture apart ~~in~~ on the lines. Now you have the pieces of a puzzle! Can you put them together again to make the picture?

fixed preposition

added exclamation point

added question mark

Reflect

Is Max's draft easier to read with the correct punctuation?

Apply

Check the punctuation and prepositions in your draft.

Punctuation

Know the Rule

End a telling sentence with a **period**. End an asking sentence with a **question mark**. End a sentence that shows strong emotion with an **exclamation point**.

Practice the Rule

Number a sheet of paper 1–8. Write each sentence with the correct end punctuation.

1. Do you like to fly a kite
2. It's so much fun
3. You can buy a kite
4. You can also make your own
5. The craft store has kits
6. Many people fly kites in the park
7. Do you want to see
8. Let's go

Prepositional Phrases

Know the Rule

Prepositional phrases help tell where things are. They begin with a preposition and end with a noun.

Examples:

by the table　　in the park　　on the lake

Practice the Rule

Number a sheet of paper 1–8. Write the prepositional phrase you find in each sentence.

1. I see the sun in the sky.
2. Is my pencil under the desk?
3. The pan is on the stove.
4. The plane flew above the clouds.
5. Please put my bag by the door.
6. Can you see the eggs in the nest?
7. The horse jumped over the fence.
8. My best friend lives down the street.

Publish

+Presentation

Publishing Strategy Publish the paper on the school website.

Presentation Strategy Use neat word processing.

Now my how-to paper is done! I'll make a final copy to share with others. I'll type my paper on the computer. The fonts I use must be clear. I'll post my paper on our school's website with my teacher's help. I'll use this checklist to publish my how-to paper. You can use it to check your final draft, too.

My Final Checklist

Did I —

✔ punctuate sentences correctly?

✔ use the correct prepositions?

✔ choose clear fonts?

FINAL DRAFT

How to Make a Jigsaw Puzzle

by Max

Have you ever made a jigsaw puzzle? I have. I'll tell you how to do it. First, find a colorful picture in a magazine. Pictures of the outdoors work best. Then, cut a piece of heavy paper so it's the same size as the picture. Next, paste the picture on the heavy paper. Let the paste dry. Draw two wavy lines across and two wavy lines down the back of the paper. Finally, cut the picture apart on the lines. Now you have the pieces of a puzzle! Can you put them together again to make the picture?

Reflect

Use the rubric to check Max's draft and your draft, too.

Parts of a Compare-and-Contrast Paper

A compare-and-contrast paper tells how two things are alike and different.

Introduction
The introduction is the beginning of the paper. It tells what two things I will compare and contrast.

Comparison
In my paper, I will tell how my two topics are alike. I could say that a cat and a dog are both pets.

Topics
A compare-and-contrast paper has two topics. I'll describe each one.

Contrast
In my paper, I will tell how my two topics are different. I could say that a dog can catch a ball but a cat can't.

Conclusion
The conclusion is the end of the paper. It sums up my main points.

Reasons for Writing a Compare-and-Contrast Paper

Here are some reasons to write a compare-and-contrast paper.

To decide
If I want to decide between two things, writing about how they are alike and how they are different can help me choose.

To convince
My sister wanted a cat, but I wanted a dog. I wrote a compare-and-contrast paper to show why I thought a dog would be better. My sister agreed!

To explain
Sometimes it's easier to understand one thing when you compare it to something else.

Linking Informative/Explanatory Writing Traits to a Compare-and-Contrast Paper

In this chapter, you will write a compare-and-contrast paper. Max will guide you through the stages of the writing process. He will also show you some writing strategies that are linked to the Informative/Explanatory Writing Traits below.

Informative/Explanatory Writing Traits

Ideas	• a clear, focused topic • accurate and complete supporting details
Organization	• a strong introduction, body, and conclusion • facts that develop the topic • transitions that connect ideas
Voice	• a voice that connects directly to the reader
Word Choice	• exact words
Sentence Fluency	• different types of sentences for variety
Conventions	• no or few errors in spelling, punctuation, and capitalization

Let's look at this model of a compare-and-contrast paper. Nora compares a movie theater and a classroom. We can use the rubric to check her writing.

Compare & Contrast Paper MODEL

A Movie Theater and a Classroom
by Nora Hernandez

introduction

two topics

A movie theater and a classroom are alike and different in many ways.

Here is how they are alike. People sit down in both places and they watch the front of the room. They look at a big screen or a big chalkboard.

comparison

contrast

Here is how the two places are different. A movie theater is dark and quiet. Everyone watches the movie. A classroom is lit up. It is noisy! People of all ages may go to the same movie theater. A classroom usually has people who are the same age. A classroom has a teacher, but a movie theater doesn't.

Classrooms and movie theaters are the same but different!

conclusion

Compare-and-Contrast Paper Rubric

	6	5	4
Ideas	The writer stays focused on comparing two topics. Accurate facts develop the topics.	The writer compares two topics. Facts are clear.	The writer compares two topics. Many facts are clear.
Organization	Topics are clearly introduced at the beginning, facts are well organized, and the conclusion is satisfying.	Topics are clearly introduced at the beginning, facts are organized, and there is a conclusion.	There is a beginning, a middle with facts, and a conclusion.
Voice	The writer's voice is perfect for the audience and purpose.	The writer's voice is formal most of the time.	The writer's voice starts out formal but fades in the middle.
Word Choice	The writer uses descriptive words that clearly show the comparison or contrast.	The writer uses words that compare and contrast.	The writer uses some words that compare and contrast.
Sentence Fluency	The writer uses a perfect combination of long and short sentences to make the writing smooth.	Short sentences are combined to make the writing smooth.	More short sentences could be combined to make smooth sentences.
Conventions	The writer forms plural and proper nouns correctly.	The writing contains minimal errors with plural and proper nouns.	A few errors with plural and proper nouns can be corrected easily.

+Presentation Paragraphs are indented.

What makes a good compare-and-contrast paper? A rubric can help you decide. Use it to help you write. Then use it again to check your writing.

3	2	1	
The writer compares two topics. More facts are needed to be clear.	The writer tells only how the topics are alike. Many facts are not accurate.	Facts are missing or incomplete.	Ideas
Either the beginning or the conclusion is missing. The facts are not well organized.	There is no clear beginning or conclusion. The piece just begins and ends.	The writing is not organized at all.	Organization
The writer's voice comes and goes.	The writer's voice is not appropriate for the audience and purpose.	There is no voice in the writing.	Voice
More words that compare and contrast are needed.	Words that make comparisons are not used.	It is hard to picture what the writer is comparing as the words are vague and unrelated.	Word Choice
Short sentences have not been combined. The writing is choppy.	The writing is hard to follow and read because the sentences are all the same length.	Many sentences are incomplete.	Sentence Fluency
Many errors with plural and proper nouns make the reader struggle to understand.	Many serious errors with plural and proper nouns leave the reader confused.	The paper has not been edited.	Conventions

See Appendix B for 4-, 5-, and 6-point Informative/Explanatory rubrics.

Compare-and-Contrast Paper

Using the Rubric to Study the Model

Let's use the rubric to check Nora's paper about a movie theater and a classroom.

Ideas

- The writer stays focused on comparing two topics.
- Accurate facts develop the topics.

The introduction tells the reader right away what the paper will be about. The focus will be comparing and contrasting a movie theater and a classroom.

A movie theater and a classroom are alike and different in many ways.

Organization

- Topics are clearly introduced at the beginning, facts are well organized, and the conclusion is satisfying.

The information is well organized. First, the paper describes the ways that a movie theater and a classroom are alike. Then it describes how they are different. The contrasts begin like this:

> Here is how the two places are different.

Voice

- The writer's voice is perfect for the audience and purpose.

The purpose of Nora's paper is to give information. Her words are not casual. Here is one example that describes a difference:

> People of all ages may go to the same movie theater. A classroom usually has people who are the same age.

Word Choice

- The writer uses descriptive words that clearly show the comparison or contrast.

Nora uses clear words to describe the movie theater and the classroom. The words *dark* and *quiet* describe the movie theater. The words *lit up* and *noisy* tell about the classroom.

> A movie theater is dark and quiet. Everyone watches the movie. A classroom is lit up. It is noisy!

Sentence Fluency

- The writer uses a perfect combination of long and short sentences to make the writing smooth.

Nora's writing is smooth. She uses both short and long sentences in her writing.

> Here is how they are alike. People sit down in both places and they watch the front of the room.

Conventions

- The writer forms plural and proper nouns correctly.

The only proper noun in Nora's paper is her name. She remembered to capitalize her name. Her paper has many plural nouns. All the plural nouns are formed correctly.

Classrooms and movie theaters are the same but different!

+Presentation Paragraphs are indented.

My Turn!

Now it's my turn. I'm going to write my own compare-and-contrast paper. Keep reading to see how I will do it.

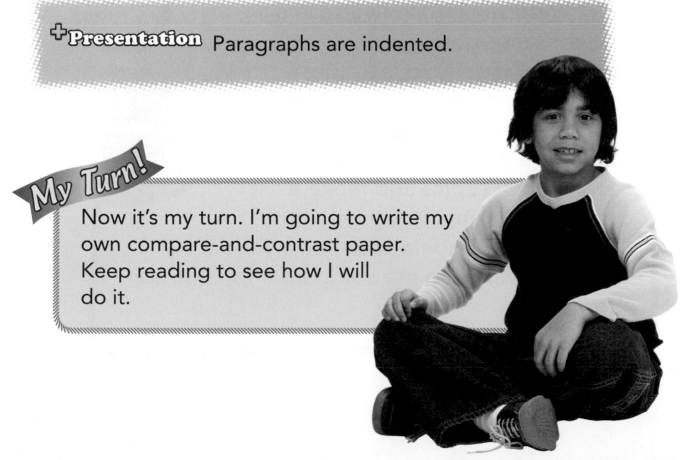

Prewrite

Focus on **Ideas**

The Rubric Says The writer stays focused on comparing two topics. Accurate facts develop the topics.

Writing Strategy Choose two things to compare and contrast. Make lists of what you know about each one.

I need to choose two topics to compare before I can start writing. I want to pick topics that are interesting. The topics must have enough details to compare and contrast. I will choose my topics and make a list about each one. I may go to the library to find some facts for my lists. The lists will help me compare and contrast the topics.

My Lists

Goldfish	Frogs
animals	animals
orange	green
swim	swim
can't walk on land	can hop and leap
can be pets	can be pets
breathe in water	can breathe air
are quiet	croak

Reflect

Do you think Max's readers will be interested in reading about these topics?

Apply

What notes can you write about your topics?

Prewrite

Focus on **Organization**

The Rubric Says Topics are clearly introduced at the beginning, facts are well organized, and the conclusion is satisfying.

Writing Strategy Make a Venn Diagram to organize your notes.

The next step is to look at the information on my lists. Then I can see how my two topics are alike and how they are different. I'll make a Venn Diagram to organize my lists about goldfish and frogs.

Writer's Term

Venn Diagram

A **Venn Diagram** is made of two circles. The circles help you show how two things are alike and different.

Graphic Organizer: Venn Diagram

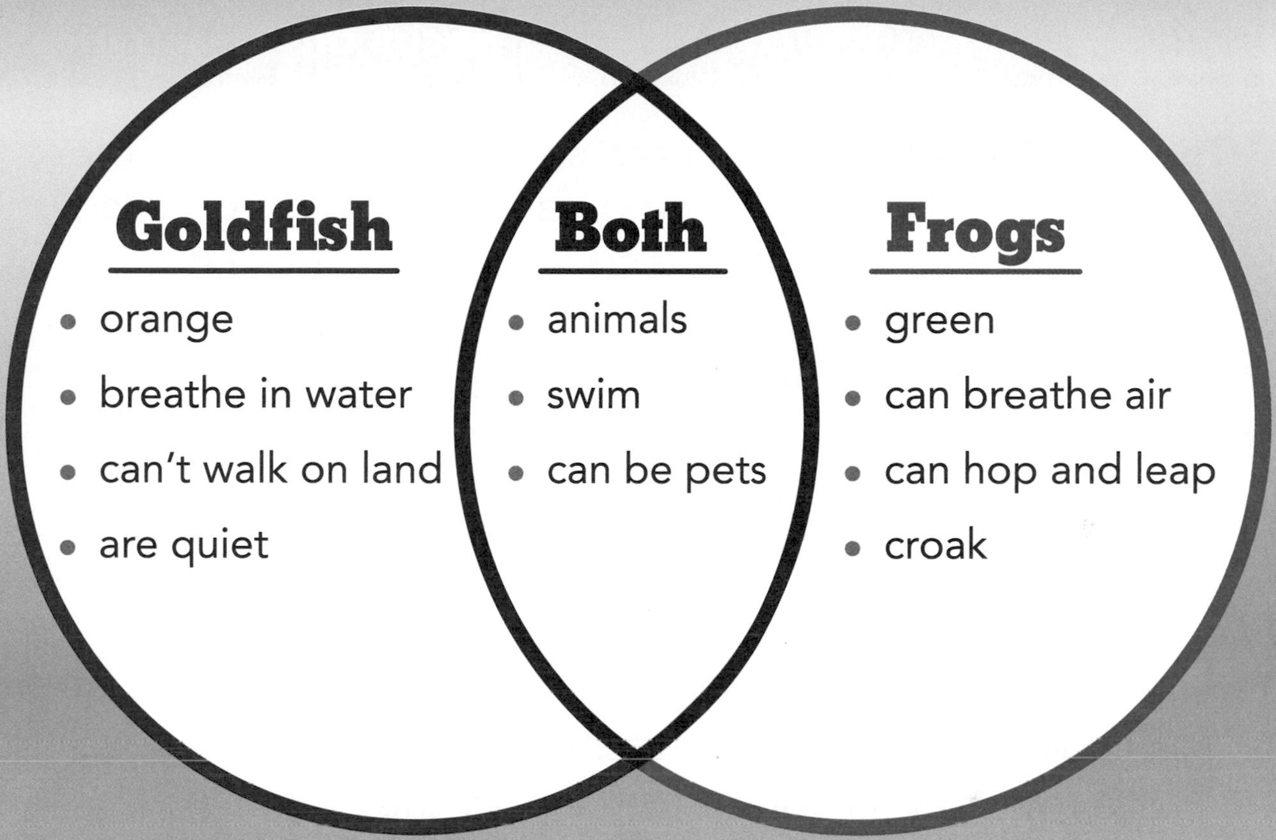

Reflect

How will a Venn Diagram help Max compare and contrast his topics?

Apply

Use your notes to make a Venn Diagram.

Draft

Focus on Organization

The Rubric Says Topics are clearly introduced at the beginning, facts are well organized, and the conclusion is satisfying.

Writing Strategy Use the Venn Diagram to organize the paper.

Now I will start writing my paper. I'll introduce the topic right away. First, I'll use the ideas in the middle of my Venn Diagram to tell how the animals are alike. Next, I'll use the left and right sections of my Venn Diagram to tell how the two animals are different. Later, I will write a conclusion.

Proofreading Marks

/ Make a small letter	∧ Add something
ℓ Take out something	⊙ Add a period
≡ Make a capital letter	

[DRAFT]

Goldfish and frogs are alike in some ways. Both are animals. Both can swim. Both goldfish and frogs can be pets you know.

comparison

Goldfish and frogs are also different. Most goldfish are orange. Most frog are green. Goldfish cant breathe out of water. Frogs can breathe air. Goldfish can't walk. Frogs can hop and leap. Goldfish are quiet, but frogs can croak loudly.

contrast

Reflect

Can you think of other ways that Max's topics are alike and different?

Apply

Now you try it. Look at your topic lists and your Venn Diagram. Start your draft.

Revise

Focus on Voice

The Rubric Says The writer's voice is perfect for the audience and purpose.

Writing Strategy Take out or replace casual language.

My writing voice is how the paper sounds. I will read my paper to see how my voice sounds. My audience is my teacher, my classmates, and people I don't know. My purpose is to give information. I need to sound like I know all about my topics. I will use a formal voice. If I see any casual language, I will take it out or replace it. Casual language is what I use to talk to my friends.

Writer's Term

Formal Voice

Formal voice is the kind of language you would use with adults, especially ones you don't know very well.

[DRAFT]

took out casual language

Goldfish and frogs are alike in some ways. Both are animals. Both can swim. Both goldfish and frogs can be pets ~~you know~~!

Goldfish and frogs are also different. Most goldfish are orange. Most frog are green. Goldfish can't breathe out of water. Frogs can breath air. Goldfish can't walk.

Reflect

Max revised one sentence in his draft. Is there any other place where Max could make his voice stronger?

Apply

Now look at your draft for places where you can make your writing more formal by replacing or taking out casual language.

Revise

Focus on Word Choice

The Rubric Says The writer uses descriptive words that clearly show the comparison or contrast.

Writing Strategy Add descriptive words.

I will read my paper again to see if I followed the rubric. It says that I should use descriptive words. Descriptive words will help my readers picture my topics. That will help them see how the topics are the same and different.

[DRAFT]

added descriptive word

Goldfish and frogs are also different. Most goldfish are shiny and golden orange. Most frog are green. Goldfish can't breathe out of water. Frogs can breathe air. Goldfish can't walk. Frogs can hop and leap. Goldfish are quiet, but frogs can croak loudly.

added descriptive words

Reflect

Do the descriptive words Max added help you see how the animals are different?

Apply

Look at your draft. Look for places to add descriptive words that will help readers see how your topics are the same and different.

Edit

Focus on Conventions

The Rubric Says The writer forms plural and proper nouns correctly.

Writing Strategy Make sure plural and proper nouns are correct.

Next I will edit my compare-and-contrast paper. That means fixing any mistakes. The rubric says to write plural and proper nouns correctly. The only proper noun in my paper will be my name. But there are other nouns that I should check.

Writer's Term

Plural and Proper Nouns

A **plural noun** names more than one person, place, or thing. (**frogs, animals**). The plural form of most nouns is created by adding *-s* to the singular form.
A **proper noun** names a particular person, place, or thing. (**Nora, Max, New Mexico**).
A proper noun starts with a capital letter.

[DRAFT]

Goldfish and frogs are also different. Most goldfish are shiny and golden orange. Most frogs are green. Goldfish sleep with open eyes because they can't close them. Frogs sleep with closed eyes. Goldfish can't breathe out of water, but Frogs can breathe air. Goldfish can't walk. Frogs can hop and leap. Goldfish are quiet, but frogs can croak loudly.

made noun plural

Reflect

Did Max do what the rubric said to do? Did he fix all his mistakes?

Apply

Now check the draft of your compare-and-contrast paper. Make sure all plural and proper nouns are written correctly.

Singular and Plural Nouns

Know the Rule

A **singular noun** names one person, place, or thing. A **plural noun** names more than one person, place, or thing. Many plural nouns are formed by adding *-s* to the end of the singular noun, as in *cats*. However, some plural nouns have irregular forms.

Examples: child—children mouse—mice
tooth—teeth fish—fish

Practice the Rule

Number a sheet of paper 1–6. Write the plural form of each underlined noun.

1. Lisa likes to play with her <u>dog</u>.
2. The <u>child</u> ran on the playground.
3. Ron fed his <u>goldfish</u>.
4. Juan put on his <u>mitten</u>.
5. Did you read the story about the cute <u>mouse</u>?
6. The dentist checked my <u>tooth</u>.

Proper Nouns

Know the Rule

A **proper noun** names a certain person, place, or thing. A proper noun begins with a capital letter.

Examples:
Isabella, Carlos (people)
Rocky Mountains, Carroll Park,
Linwood Street, Oak Hills School (places)
Golden Gate Bridge, Statue of Liberty (things)

Practice the Rule

Number a sheet of paper 1–6. Copy each sentence. Capitalize the proper noun in the sentence.

1. Is millie coming to the party?
2. This bus is going to boston.
3. Let's walk down church street.
4. Did you see all the flowers in green park?
5. I want to visit mt. rushmore some day.
6. This book is about abraham lincoln.

Publish

+Presentation

Publishing Strategy Add the paper to the class book.

Presentation Strategy Indent each paragraph.

My paper is finished! Now I am ready to publish it in a class book. I'll use this checklist to make sure that I don't forget anything. I will make sure the ideas are grouped together in paragraphs. An indented line shows the beginning of each paragraph. You can use the checklist for your paper, too.

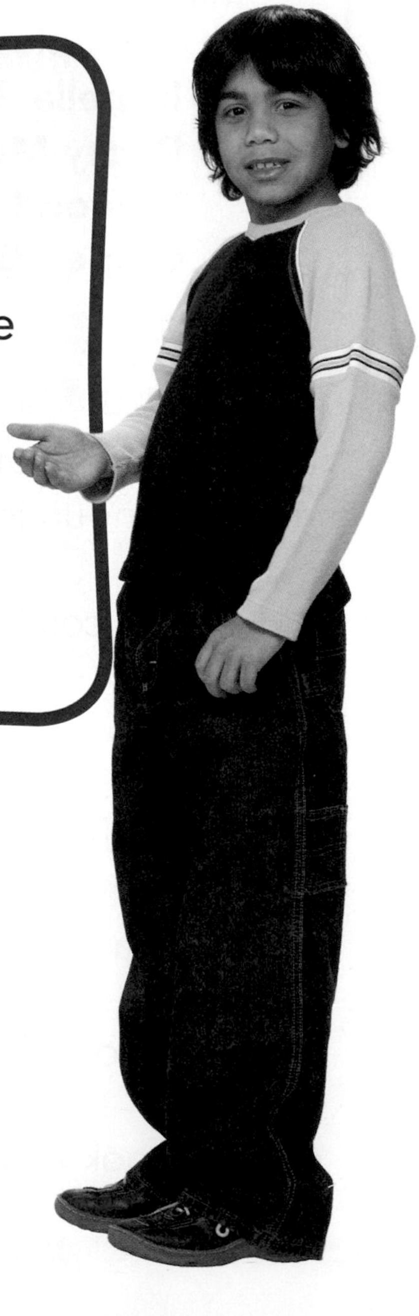

My Final Checklist

Did I —

- ✔ start each proper noun with a capital letter?
- ✔ form plural nouns correctly?
- ✔ indent each paragraph?

FINAL DRAFT

Goldfish and Frogs

by Max

Goldfish and frogs are alike in some ways. Both are animals. Both can swim. Both goldfish and frogs can be pets.

Goldfish and frogs are also different. Most goldfish are shiny and golden orange. Most frogs are green. Goldfish sleep with open eyes because they can't close them. Frogs sleep with closed eyes. Goldfish can't breathe out of water, but frogs can breathe air. Goldfish can't walk. Frogs can hop and leap. Goldfish are quiet, but frogs can croak loudly.

As you can see, there are several ways that goldfish and frogs are alike and different.

Reflect

Use the rubric to check Max's paper and your own.

Parts of a Research Report

A research report tells facts about a topic. It can be about anything that interests me. It can be about a person, a place, a thing, an event, or something else!

Topic
The topic is what the report is about. The topic can be almost anything, such as butterflies, a special person, or the Olympics.

Facts
A fact is something that can be proved. I can prove how tall I am because I can be measured. I can't prove that my favorite music sounds beautiful. Some people may not like my music.

Introduction
This is the beginning of the report. I tell the topic of my paper and catch the reader's attention in this part.

Body
This is the longest part of the report. I tell facts about my topic in this part.

Conclusion
This is the end of the report. I sum up the main point of my report in this part.

Reasons for Writing a Research Report

Here are some reasons to write a research report.

To share information

When I learn something new or important, I like to tell others about it in a research report. Then they can learn about it, too.

To answer questions

A research report is a great way to answer questions I have about something. I can look in books to find answers. Then I can tell what I have learned.

To entertain

I can make my topic interesting for the reader by including unusual or surprising facts. I can tell about an event that the reader might like to experience.

Linking Informative/Explanatory Writing Traits to a Research Report

In this chapter, you will write a research report. Max will guide you through the stages of the writing process. He will also show you some writing strategies that are linked to the Informative/Explanatory Writing Traits below.

Informative/Explanatory Writing Traits

Ideas	• a clear, focused topic • accurate and complete supporting details
Organization	• a strong introduction, body, and conclusion • facts that develop the topic • transitions that connect ideas
Voice	• a voice that connects directly to the reader
Word Choice	• exact words
Sentence Fluency	• different types of sentences for variety
Conventions	• no or few errors in spelling, punctuation, and capitalization

Let's look at this model of a research report. Josh tells a lot of interesting facts about rocks. We will use the rubric on the next two pages to check his writing.

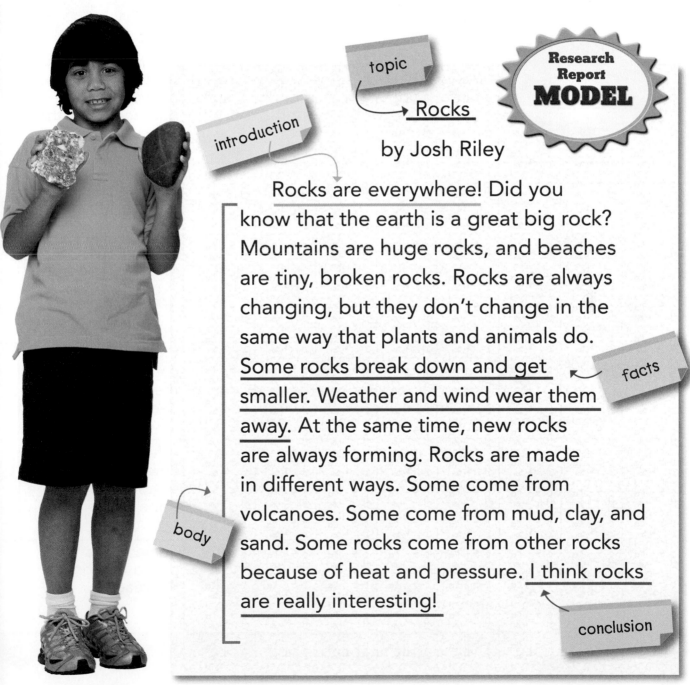

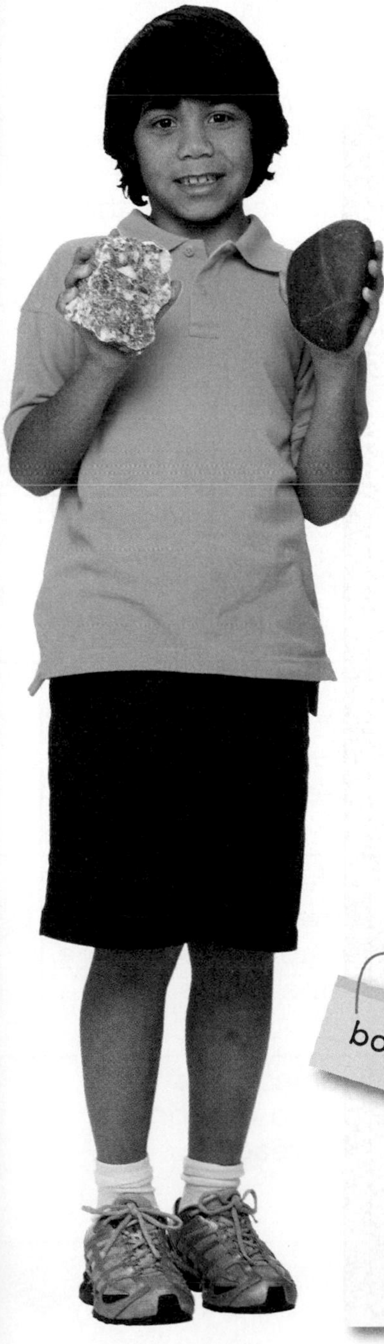

Research Report MODEL

topic

Rocks

introduction

by Josh Riley

Rocks are everywhere! Did you know that the earth is a great big rock? Mountains are huge rocks, and beaches are tiny, broken rocks. Rocks are always changing, but they don't change in the same way that plants and animals do. Some rocks break down and get smaller. Weather and wind wear them away. At the same time, new rocks are always forming. Rocks are made in different ways. Some come from volcanoes. Some come from mud, clay, and sand. Some rocks come from other rocks because of heat and pressure. I think rocks are really interesting!

facts

body

conclusion

Research Report Rubric

	6	5	4
Ideas	The report uses facts to develop an interesting topic and answers all questions completely.	Facts develop the topic. The report answers questions about the topic.	A few facts develop the topic. The report answers only one question about the topic.
Organization	The writer presents facts in perfect order. The conclusion wraps up the writing.	The details are in order. There is a conclusion.	Most details are in order. There is a conclusion.
Voice	The writer uses a clear voice and sounds like an expert on the topic.	The writer usually sounds like an expert on the topic.	The writer sounds like an expert most of the time.
Word Choice	The word choice is precise and clear. The writer defines content-specific words.	Words are used correctly. Specific words are explained for the reader.	Words are used correctly most of the time. A few may need explanations.
Sentence Fluency	All sentences are smooth. They are easy to read and follow.	A couple of sentences begin the same way, but the writing is smooth.	A few sentences flow smoothly. Some sentences begin the same way.
Conventions	Sentences use pronouns correctly to create understanding.	A few errors with pronouns can be easily corrected.	Some errors with pronouns confuse the reader.

+Presentation The report is neat and legible.

What makes a good research report? A rubric can help you decide. Use it to help you write. Then use it again to check your writing.

	3	2	1
Ideas	Facts are weak or incorrect. The report does not answer questions about the topic.	The report is confusing and the reader struggles to understand.	The topic of the report is not clear.
Organization	The details are confusing. There is no conclusion.	The details are incomplete. Some may be missing.	The details do not help explain a topic.
Voice	The writer sounds like an expert some of the time.	The writer sounds like an expert in the beginning.	The writer does not sound like an expert.
Word Choice	Some words are used incorrectly. No specific words are explained.	Many words are repeated or used incorrectly. The reader may be confused.	The word choice seems random or accidental. The reader is confused.
Sentence Fluency	Many sentences begin the same way. The reader may lose interest.	Many sentences are repetitive and choppy. The reader could be confused and uninterested.	Sentences are incomplete. The sentences do not explain a topic.
Conventions	Many errors with pronouns make the reader struggle to understand.	Numerous errors with pronouns prevent understanding.	Serious, frequent errors with pronouns make the writing hard to understand.

See Appendix B for 4-, 5-, and 6-point research report rubrics.

Using the Research Report Rubric to Study the Model

Let's use the rubric to check Josh's research report about rocks.

Ideas

- The report uses facts to develop an interesting topic and answer all questions completely.

Josh's report tells many facts about rocks. He makes his topic sound very interesting right from the beginning. The first two sentences of his report make the reader want to learn more!

> Rocks are everywhere! Did you know that the earth is a great big rock?

Organization

- The writer presents facts in perfect order.
- The conclusion wraps up the writing.

The order of the facts in the report makes sense. First, Josh tells all about how rocks change. Then he tells how rocks are made. The last sentence tells how Josh feels about the topic.

> I think rocks are really interesting!

Voice

- The writer uses a clear voice and sounds like an expert on the topic.

All through his paper, Josh really sounds like he knows what he is writing about. The facts he tells are very clear. His writer's voice sounds formal.

> Rocks are made in different ways. Some come from volcanoes. Some come from mud, clay, and sand.

Word Choice • The word choice is precise and clear.

Josh is very precise and clear in his choice of words. This helps the reader understand what he is saying. Here, he explains how rocks break down:

> Some rocks break down and get smaller. Weather and wind wear them away.

Sentence Fluency • All sentences are smooth. They are easy to read and follow.

Josh's writing is easy to follow, even when a sentence is long. Here's an example of a long sentence that is easy to read:

> Mountains are huge rocks, and beaches are tiny, broken rocks.

Conventions • Sentences use pronouns correctly to create understanding.

Josh uses the pronoun *they*. This pronoun takes the place of the word *rocks*. Imagine if Josh had used the word *rocks* again in the same sentence!

Rocks are always changing, but they don't change in the same way that plants and animals do.

+Presentation The report is neat and legible.

My Turn!

Now it's my turn. I'm going to write my own research report. Read on to see how I will do it.

Prewrite

Focus on **Ideas**

The Rubric Says The report uses facts to develop an interesting topic and answer all questions completely.

Writing Strategy Choose a topic. Write questions and notes about the topic.

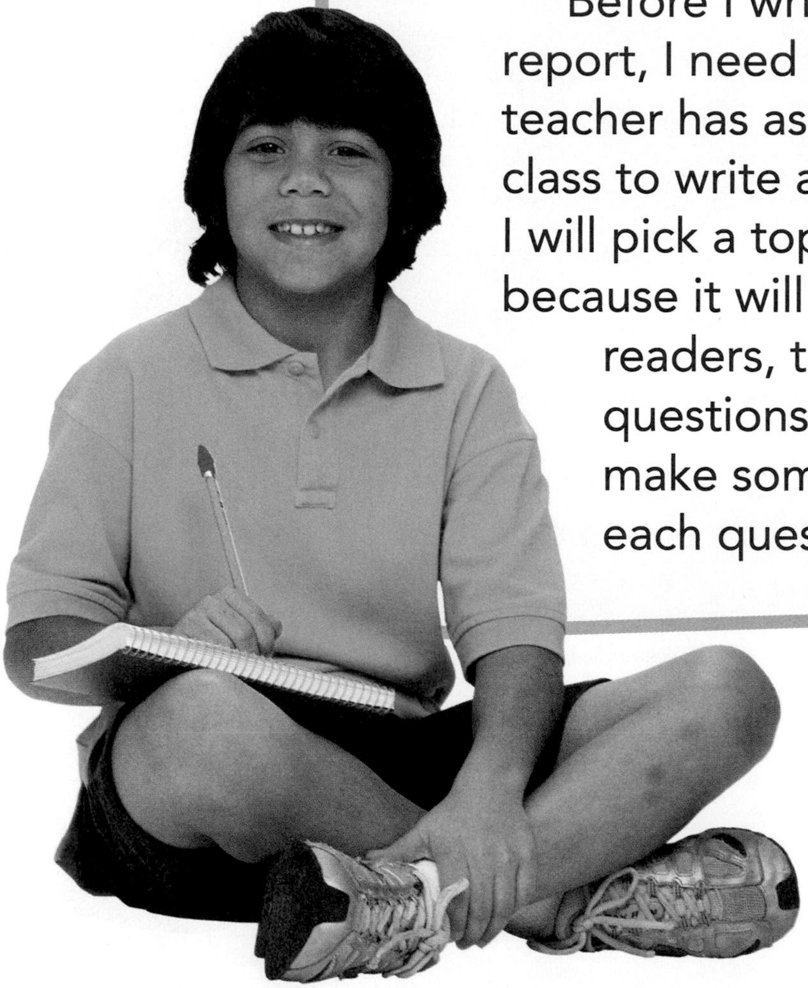

Before I write my research report, I need to pick a topic. My teacher has asked everyone in the class to write about a science topic. I will pick a topic that interests me because it will probably interest my readers, too! Then I'll write two questions about the topic and make some notes that answer each question.

My First Question

What are clouds?

My Second Question

How do clouds change the weather?

My Notes

- Clouds have billions of bits of water.
- Clouds give us rain and snow.
- Water drops fall as rain.
- Some clouds are made of ice crystals.
- Some clouds are made of water drops.
- Ice crystals fall as snow.
- Rain and sun make rainbows!
- Clouds float because the water in them is lighter than the air.

Reflect

Did Max follow the rubric? Do you think Max chose an interesting topic?

Apply

Choose a topic. Write two questions. Then write notes to answer the questions.

Prewrite

Focus on Organization

The Rubric Says The writer presents facts in perfect order.

Writing Strategy Make a Web for each of the questions.

The rubric says that the writer should present the facts in perfect order. I'll make a Web. It will help me organize the facts. I can put facts that go together in the same part of the Web. I'll use the Web to write my paper. First, I'll tell information about what clouds are. Then I'll tell how clouds change the weather.

Writer's Term

Web

A **Web** shows information about a topic. The topic is in the middle. Information surrounds the topic.

Graphic Organizer: Web

Topic: Clouds

Question 1: What are clouds?

- **Fact 1:** ice crystals or water drops
- **Fact 2:** billions of bits of water
- **Fact 3:** float because they are lighter than air

Question 2: How do clouds change the weather?

- **Fact 1:** make snow from ice crystals
- **Fact 2:** make rainbows
- **Fact 3:** make rain from water drops

Reflect

Did Max organize his information so that it makes sense?

Apply

Write your topic and questions in a Web. Put the notes in the Web where they belong.

Draft

Focus on Word Choice

The Rubric Says The word choice is precise and clear.

Writing Strategy Use exact words.

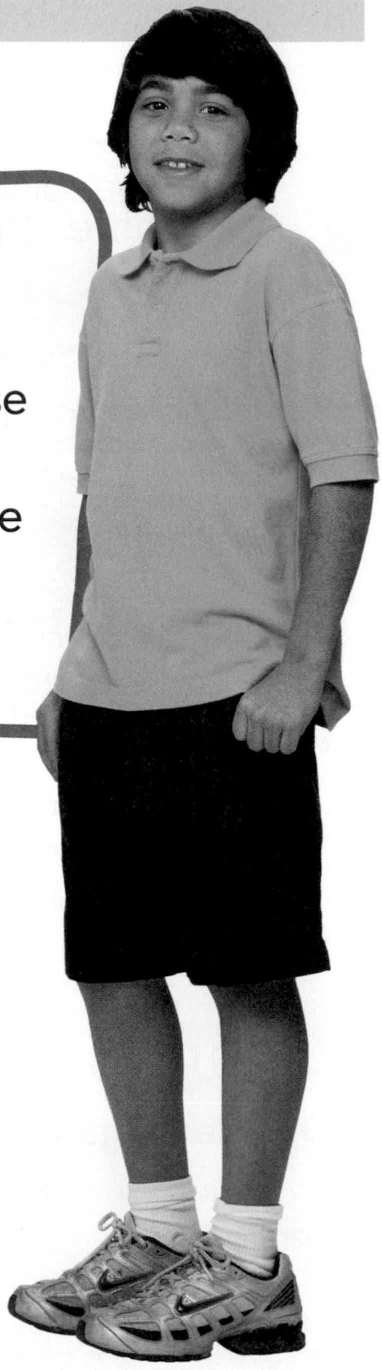

When writing about science, the writer should use exact words. Exact words will make the concept clear. I'll use my Web to organize my draft. Then I'll include exact words. If I can't think of the right word now, I'll make a note. Later I can find the right word.

Proofreading Marks

/ Make a small letter	∧ Add something
ℓ Take out something	⊙ Add a period
≡ Make a capital letter	

[DRAFT]

Clouds are made of billions of tiny water drops. Wow, can you believe that? Clouds can also be made of ice crystals. The water drops or the ice crystals make a mist suspended in air. We see that mist as clouds. The drops and crystals float because it are lighter than air. Clouds give us rain and snow. Both rain and snow begin as ice crystals. Some ice crystals fall as snow. Other ice crystals become water drops. They fall as rain. Clouds also give us rainbows.

exact words

exact words

Reflect

Did Max use exact words?

Apply

Now you try it. Look at your topic and your Web. Start your first draft.

Revise

Focus on **Voice**

The Rubric Says	The writer uses a clear voice and sounds like an expert on the topic.
Writing Strategy	Use a formal voice and sound like an expert.

Voice is the way writing sounds. Voice should fit the audience and the purpose. The audience is my teacher and classmates. The purpose is to explain clouds. My writer's voice should sound formal and like I am an expert on the topic. I'll check my draft to make sure my voice is formal all the way through.

Writer's Term

Formal Language

Formal Language is the kind of language used when talking to adults, especially ones you do not know well.

[DRAFT]

took out casual comment

Clouds are made of billions of tiny water drops. ~~Wow, can you believe that?~~ Clouds can also be made of ice crystals. The water drops or the ice crystals make a mist suspended in air. We see that mist as clouds. The drops and crystals float because it are lighter than air. Clouds give us rain and snow. Both rain and snow begin as ice crystals. Some ice crystals fall as snow. Other ice crystals become water drops. They fall as rain. Clouds also give us rainbows.

Reflect

Does the voice in Max's report sound more formal after he made his revision?

Apply

Is the language formal throughout your draft? Is there any casual language you should change?

Revise

Focus on Sentence Fluency

The Rubric Says All sentences are smooth. They are easy to read and follow.

Writing Strategy Start sentences in different ways.

I'll read my report again to make sure I've followed the rubric. It says that my sentences should be smooth and easy to follow.

If too many sentences start the same way, my writing will sound choppy. Many of my sentences start with *clouds*. I'll use a pronoun to start a sentence instead. That will make the sentences smoother.

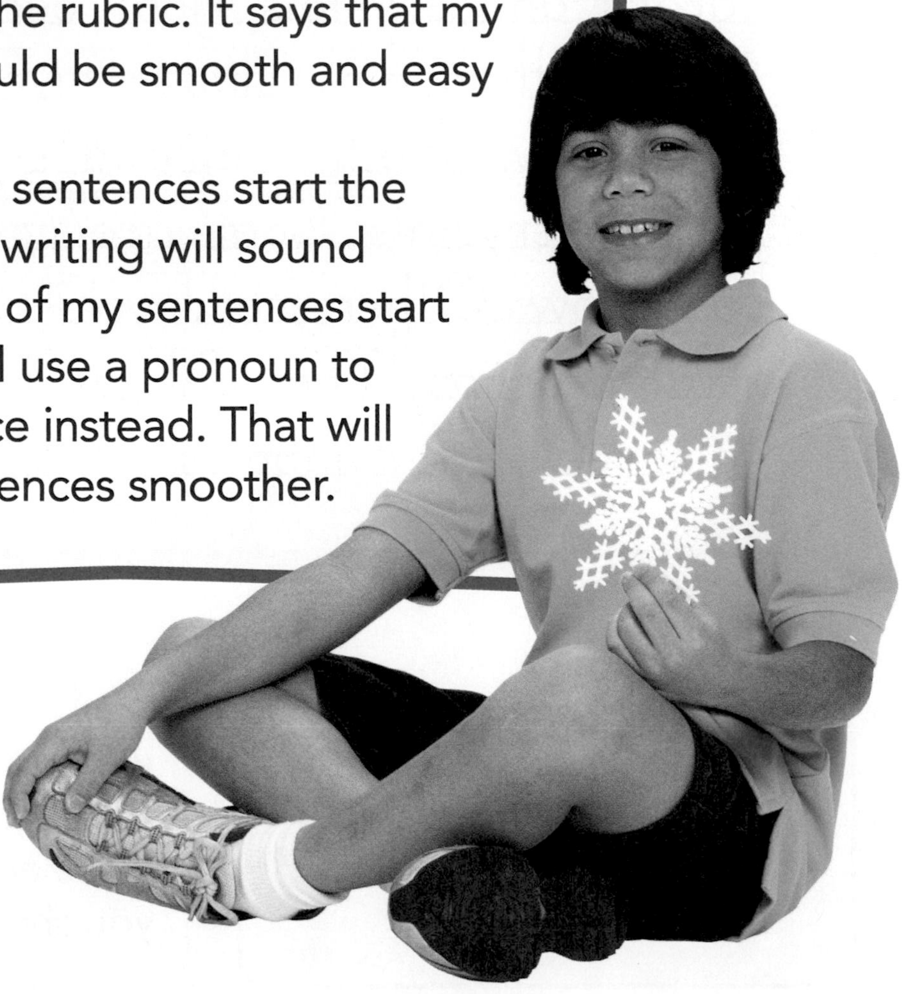

[DRAFT]

varied beginning of sentence

Clouds are made of billions of tiny water drops. ~~Wow, can you believe that?~~ ~~Clouds~~ They can also be made of ice crystals. The water drops or the ice crystals make a mist suspended in air. We see that mist as clouds. The drops and crystals float because it are lighter than air. Clouds give us rain and snow. Both rain and snow begin as ice crystals. Some ice crystals fall as snow. Other ice crystals become water drops. They fall as rain. Clouds also give us rainbows.

Reflect

Do Max's sentences flow? Did he make a good change?

Apply

Look at your draft. Check to see if there are sentences that begin the same way. Change one or two of them.

Edit

Focus on **Conventions**

The Rubric Says Sentences use pronouns correctly to create understanding.

Writing Strategy Use pronouns correctly.

Next I'll edit my report. This is when I check my sentences for capital letters and end marks. I also check my spelling. The rubric says to make sure to use pronouns correctly. If I use the wrong pronoun, my readers will be confused.

Writer's Term

Pronouns

Pronouns take the place of nouns. Common pronouns are **I, me, you, he,** and **she.**

[DRAFT]

Clouds are made of billions of tiny water drops. ~~Wow, can you believe that?~~ ~~Clouds~~ They can also be made of ice crystals. The water drops or the ice crystals make a mist suspended, or hanging, in air. We see that mist as clouds. The drops and crystals float because ~~it~~ they are lighter than air. Clouds give us rain and snow. Both rain and snow begin as ice crystals. Some ice crystals fall as snow. Other ice crystals become water drops. Water drops in clouds can get big and heavy.

corrected a pronoun

Reflect

Did Max use pronouns correctly?

Apply

Now check your own draft. Make sure pronouns are used correctly.

Personal Pronouns

Know the Rule

A **personal pronoun** takes the place of one or more nouns. Use these pronouns as the subject in a sentence: *I, you, he, she, it, we,* and *they.*

Example: Hakim rides the bus. **He** sits next to Rita.

Practice the Rule

Number a sheet of paper 1–8. Write the pronoun that completes each sentence.

1. Uncle Bob is coming to visit. (He/She) lives in Ohio.
2. Zoe and Liam love baseball. (You/They) practice every day.
3. The sun is shining. (It/He) is high in the sky.
4. Annie is a great skater. (He/She) has won many prizes.
5. Read this book, Eve. (You/They) will like it.
6. Mom and I ate lunch early. (We/You) were hungry!
7. Jimmy plays the guitar. (He/It) plays very well.
8. My cat just had kittens. (You/They) are so cute!

Compound Personal Pronouns

Know the Rule

Use the **compound personal pronouns** *myself* and *ourselves* to speak or write about yourself. Use the compound personal pronouns *herself, itself, yourself, yourselves,* and *themselves* to refer to other people and things.

Example: Tina made **herself** a sandwich.

Practice the Rule

Number a sheet of paper 1–6. Write the pronoun that completes each sentence.

1. I set up the tent (myself/itself).
2. The fire burned (itself/themselves) out.
3. Maria wrote a story about (himself/herself).
4. We planned the party (ourselves/themselves).
5. Jake and Sam bought (themselves/yourselves) funny glasses.
6. Can you carry that chair by (myself/yourself)?

Publish

+Presentation

Publishing Strategy Read the report aloud.

Presentation Strategy Use your best handwriting or word processing.

Our teacher said that we will read our reports to the class. Later we might make a podcast to share with family and friends. My final copy should be neat so that I can read it easily. I don't want to make a mistake when I read it aloud. I'll use this checklist to check my final draft.

My Final Checklist

Did I —

✔ use all pronouns correctly?

✔ check my spelling and punctuation?

✔ write or type neatly?

FINAL DRAFT

Clouds

by Max

Clouds are made of billions of tiny water drops. They can also be made of ice crystals. The water drops or the ice crystals make a mist suspended, or hanging, in air. We see that mist as clouds. The drops and crystals float because they are lighter than air. Clouds give us rain and snow. Both rain and snow begin as ice crystals. Some ice crystals fall as snow. Other ice crystals become water drops. Water drops in clouds can get big and heavy. They fall as rain. Clouds also give us rainbows. When the sun shines through rain, we see a rainbow. Clouds are amazing!

Reflect

Be sure to use the rubric to check your final report.

Informative/ Explanatory test writing

Read the Writing Prompt

Every writing test starts with a writing prompt. Most writing prompts have three parts:

Setup This tells what you need to know to get ready for writing.

Task This tells exactly what you're supposed to write.

Scoring Guide This part tells how your writing will be scored. You should include everything on the list to do well on the test.

A scoring guide is a lot like a rubric. It lists everything you need to think about to write a good paper. Many scoring guides will have the same parts as the rubrics we've looked at:

- Ideas
- Organization
- Voice
- Word Choice
- Sentence Fluency
- Conventions

Writing MODEL Prompt

Everyone has many skills. Think about things you know how to do. You can teach others how to do one of them.

Write a how-to paper. Explain how to do something or how to make something.

Be sure your how-to paper

- has a clear topic and complete steps.
- uses time-order words.
- has a writer's voice that connects with readers.
- uses active, strong words.
- has sentences that begin with different words.
- has correct capitalization, punctuation, and spelling.

Writing Traits in the Scoring Guide

The scoring guide on page 185 has been made into this chart. How is it like the rubrics you've been using? Not all test prompts have all six writing traits. This one does!

Ideas	• **Be sure your paper has a clear topic and complete steps.**
Organization	• **Be sure your paper uses time-order words.**
Voice	• **Be sure your paper has a writer's voice that connects with readers.**
Word Choice	• **Be sure your paper uses active, strong words.**
Sentence Fluency	• **Be sure your paper has sentences that begin with different words.**
Conventions	• **Be sure your paper has correct capitalization, punctuation, and spelling.**

Look at Sidney Bohary's paper. Did he follow the scoring guide?

Writing Prompt **MODEL** Response

Shake It Up!

by Sidney Bohary

It's fun to make music with instruments you can make yourself. I can tell you how to make a musical shaker.

First, you need a container you can seal. You can use a plastic bottle, a small plastic tub, or a jar. Anything with a lid will work.

Next, you need some small, hard objects. Use dried beans, rice, gravel, or small beads. Pour some in the container.

Then put the lid on and shake. You can change the sound. Take away some of the hard things or add more.

Once you like the sound, glue on the lid. Finally, decorate your shaker. Stick on colorful pictures or paint it. Use your imagination!

Using the Scoring Guide to Study the Model

Now let's use the scoring guide to check Sidney's writing test, "Shake It Up!"

Ideas

- The paper has a clear topic and complete steps.

Sidney tells readers what the topic will be. Readers will learn how to make a shaker. The rest of his paper tells how.

I can tell you how to make a musical shaker.

Organization

- The paper uses time-order words.

Time-order words like *First, Next,* and *Then* explain the order of the steps. Read how Sidney uses time-order words.

First, you need a container you can seal. You can use a plastic bottle, a small plastic tub, or a jar. Anything with a lid will work.

Next, you need some small, hard objects.

Voice

- The paper has a voice that connects with readers.

Sidney uses the words *I, you,* and *your* to speak directly to the readers. This makes his writing friendly and personal.

Once you like the sound, glue on the lid. Finally, decorate your shaker.

Using the Scoring Guide to Study the Model

Word Choice

- The paper uses active, strong words.

Strong words help the reader understand exactly what to do. The verbs *shake, take away,* and *add* give clear information.

> Then put the lid on and shake. You can change the sound. Take away some of the hard things or add more.

Sentence Fluency

- The paper has sentences that begin with different words.

Sidney uses different words to begin his sentences. This makes his writing more interesting and enjoyable to read.

> Finally, decorate your shaker. Stick on colorful pictures or paint it. Use your imagination!

Conventions

- The capitalization, punctuation, and spelling are correct.

Be sure to look for any mistakes that you make often. Sidney did not make any mistakes at all in capitalization or punctuation. His final draft doesn't have any errors.

Many tests are timed. Your teacher will tell you how much time you have to take a test. Look on the next two pages for some tips on how to plan your time and take a test.

Planning My Time

Look at the picture of the clock. Do you see that there is more green than any other color? That means you should spend most of your time getting ready to write. What takes the least amount of time?

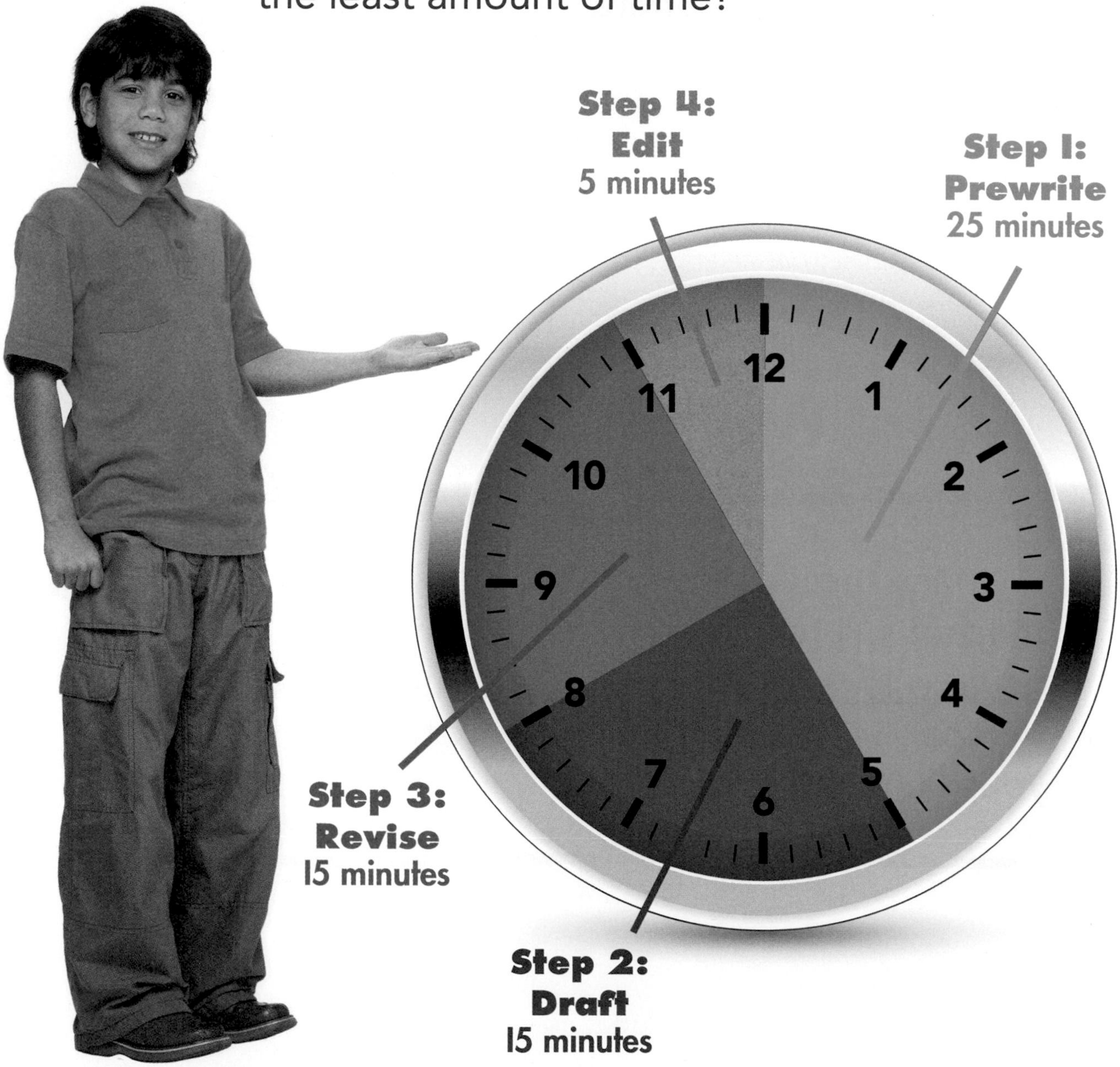

Remember these important tips when you write for a test.

Test Tips

1. Study the writing prompt before you start to write.
2. Make sure you understand the task before you start to write.
3. Keep an eye on the clock.
4. Reread your writing. Compare it to the scoring guide at least twice.
5. Plan, plan, plan!
6. Write neatly.

Prewrite

Focus on **Ideas**

Writing Strategy Study the writing prompt and choose a topic.

Getting ready to write is very important. First, I need to study the prompt. Then I will know what to do. I circled the important words in the task. These words tell me what I will write. This prompt says to write a how-to paper. My paper should tell all the steps.

Next, I need to figure out what I can write about. I have to think about something I know how to do. I taught my parakeet to talk. I will write a how-to paper about that. My paper will be about how to teach a parakeet to talk.

My Writing Test Prompt

Setup — Suppose that your class is putting together a how-to book. What things do you know how to do? What would you like to teach others?

Task — Think of something you know how to do. Write a how-to paper. Explain how to do something. Be sure to tell all the steps clearly.

Here are my notes about how to teach a parakeet to talk.

Notes

- say a word over and over again
- do this for about 15 minutes every day
- when the parakeet says the word, give it a treat

Apply

Think about a how-to paper you can write. Then jot down some notes to help you get started.

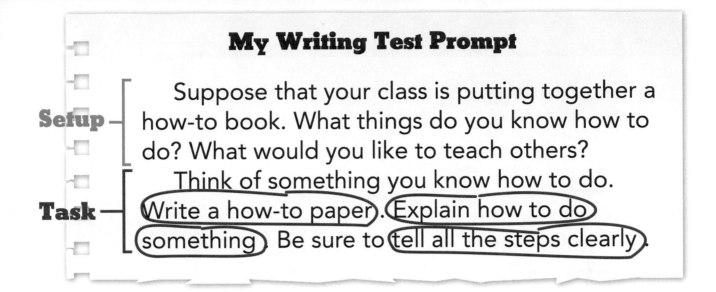

Prewrite

Focus on Organization

Writing Strategy Make a graphic organizer.

I will organize my notes. My topic is how to teach a parakeet to talk. When I tell how to do something, I need to give the steps in order. An Order Chain can help me put the steps in order. I will put the topic at the top of the chart. Then I will list the steps.

Graphic Organizer: Order Chain

Topic: How to Teach a Parakeet to Talk

First Step	Be in a quiet place.
Next Step	Choose a word to teach your bird.
Next Step	Say the word over and over again.
Next Step	Do this for 15 minutes every day.
Last Step	Give the bird a treat when it says the word.

Reflect

Look at Max's Order Chain. Will it help him write a good how-to paper?

Apply

Choose the best graphic organizer for the assignment. Organize your information.

Draft

Focus on **Ideas**

Writing Strategy Be sure your paper has a clear topic.

A how-to paper explains how to do something. First, I'll tell what the topic will be. Then readers will know what my paper is about.

I'll follow my Graphic Organizer. The topic is at the top of the chart. The steps come next.

As I write, I'll check the scoring guide. I'll follow it. This will help me to do well on my test.

Proofreading Marks

- / Make a small letter
- ∧ Add something
- ℓ Take out something
- ⊙ Add a period
- ≡ Make a capital letter

[DRAFT]

How to Teach a Parakeet to Talk
by Max

topic

You can teach your parakeet to talk. It's easy. Do these steps.

Make sure you and the bird are in a quiet place. Decide what word you want to teach. Pick a simple word. Pick a name or a greeting. Say the word. Say it over and over again.

When the paraket has said the word, give it a treat. You can teach it more words. One parakeet learned to say "Pretty bird!"

Reflect

Read the draft. Is the topic of the paper clear?

Apply

Tell what the topic of the paper will be.

Revise

Focus on Ideas

Writing Strategy Be sure your paper has complete steps.

I'll read my draft again. I want to see how I can make it better. A how-to paper tells how to do something. The information I give has to be very clear. All the steps have to be there. Every step must have all the right information. I have to make sure that I don't leave anything out.

[DRAFT]

Make sure you and the bird are in a quiet place. Decide what word you want to teach. Pick a simple word. Pick a name or a greeting. Say the word clearly. Say it over and over again. Do this for 15 minutes every day.

When the parakeet has said the word, give it a treat. You can teach it more words. One parakeet learned to say "Pretty bird!"

added information to the steps

Reflect

Look at Max's revisions. He added some information. Does this make his how-to paper clearer?

Apply

Follow the scoring guide in your own writing. Make sure your paper has complete steps.

Revise

Focus on Organization

Writing Strategy Use time-order words.

I'll read my paper again. This time I'll make sure the order of the steps is clear. I have listed the steps in order. I can make sure my readers understand the order by adding time-order words. Some time-order words are *First*, *Next*, and *Then*. They tell when to do things. I'll make my changes right on my draft.

[DRAFT]

added time-order words

First, ~~M~~ake sure you and the bird are in a quiet place. Next, ~~D~~ecide what word you want to teach. Pick a simple word. Pick a name or a greeting. Then, ~~S~~ay the word clearly. Say it over and over again. Do this for 15 minutes every day.

When the parakeet has said the word, give it a treat. Then, ~~Y~~ou can teach it more words. One parakeet learned to say "Pretty bird!"

Reflect

Look at Max's revisions. Look at the time-order words he added. Do they make the order of the steps clearer?

Apply

Check your draft. Make sure the order of steps is clear. Add time-order words.

Edit

Focus on Conventions

Writing Strategy Check the capitalization, punctuation, and spelling.

Sometimes I make spelling mistakes. My teacher told me to touch each word with my pencil. That helps me study each word carefully.

I found a spelling mistake. I misspelled parakeet one time. I fixed it.

Edits should be marked neatly. There is no chance to make a neat final copy.

FINAL DRAFT

How to Teach a Parakeet to Talk

by Max

You can teach your parakeet to talk. I did. It's easy. ~~Do~~ Follow these steps.

First, ~~M~~ake sure you and ~~the~~ your bird are in a quiet place. Next, ~~D~~ecide what word you want to teach. Pick a simple word. ~~Pick~~, like a name or a greeting. Then, ~~S~~ay the word clearly. ~~Say~~ Repeat it over and over again. Do this for 15 minutes every day.

When the parakeet has said the word, give it a treat. Then, ~~Y~~ou can teach it more words. ~~One~~ My parakeet learned to say "Pretty bird!"

Reflect

Use the scoring guide to check Max's paper and your own.

Opinion writing

tells what I think and why.

Hi! my name is Tashi. I live in Massachusetts. If you're like me, you have opinions about all kinds of things. I'm going to learn how to share what I think in writing. I'll start by writing an opinion paper.

In this unit

- Opinion Paper
- Response to Literature
- SOCIAL STUDIES CONNECTION ▶ Opinion Speech
- Writing for a Test

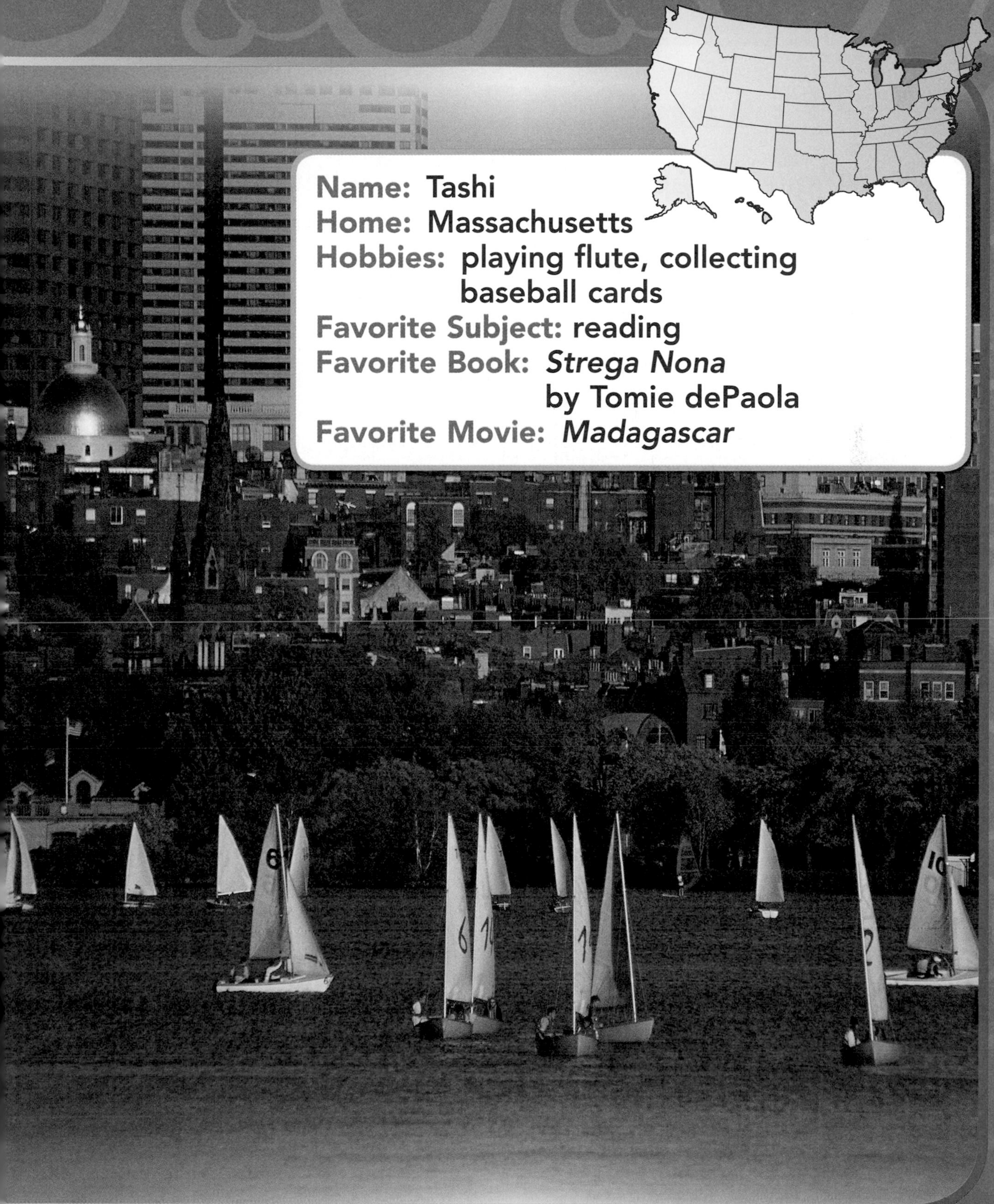

Name: Tashi
Home: Massachusetts
Hobbies: playing flute, collecting baseball cards
Favorite Subject: reading
Favorite Book: *Strega Nona* by Tomie dePaola
Favorite Movie: *Madagascar*

Parts of an Opinion Paper

An opinion paper tells the reader what I think or feel about something. I can write about something that I like, such as my favorite food. I can also write about something I disagree with or dislike.

Opinion
This is what my paper is about. It's what I think or feel about something. I give my opinion at the beginning of the paper.

Reasons
I will give reasons for why I feel the way I do about something. Reasons help to explain my opinion.

Paragraphs
A paragraph is a group of sentences. I'll use paragraphs to keep ideas that are similar together. This will make my paper easier to read.

Details
Details give more specific information. They help explain my opinion and reasons.

Reasons for Writing an Opinion Paper

Here are some reasons to write an opinion paper.

To share
I like to share my ideas with friends and family. Writing can be a good way to explain how I'm feeling. An opinion paper helps me organize my thoughts.

To convince
An opinion paper is a great way to convince someone of something. When I thought my bedtime was too early, I wrote down my reasons. My parents read my reasons and agreed to let me stay up for an extra half hour.

To entertain
An opinion paper can be entertaining. I might write that a skunk is my favorite animal. That's funny because people don't expect it, and it might make my readers think differently about skunks.

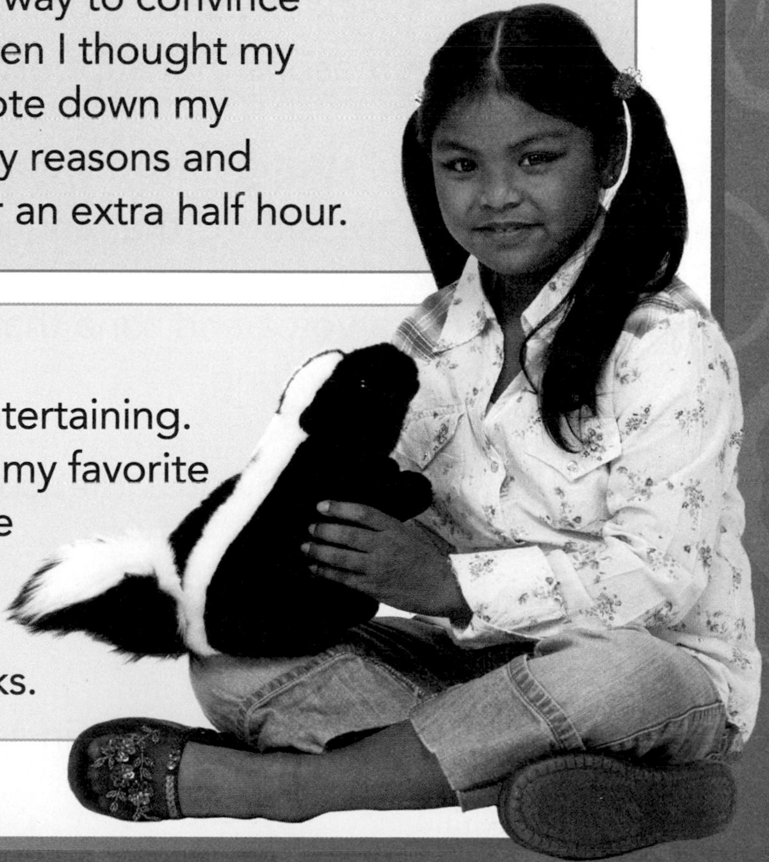

Linking Opinion Writing Traits to an Opinion Paper

In this chapter, you will write about what you think or feel about something. This type of writing is called an opinion paper. Tashi will guide you through the stages of the writing process. She will also show you some writing strategies that are linked to the Opinion Writing Traits below.

Opinion Writing Traits

Ideas	• a clearly stated opinion • reasons that support the opinion
Organization	• a strong introduction, body, and conclusion • transitions that connect opinion and reasons
Voice	• a voice and tone that are perfect for the piece of writing
Word Choice	• strong words that convince the reader
Sentence Fluency	• varied sentences
Conventions	• no or few errors in spelling, punctuation, and capitalization

Let's look at this model of an opinion paper. Mitch tells why tomato soup is his favorite meal. We can use the rubric on the next two pages to check his writing.

Opinion Paper MODEL

opinion

My Favorite Meal

by Mitch Muller

Tomato soup is the best food in the world. One reason I like it so much is that it is simple to make, since you just open a can. You pour the soup into a bowl. Then you can heat the tasty meal in a microwave.

reason

Tomato soup goes with almost everything because it tastes great. You can eat it with crackers or toast. Also, it is perfect with most sandwiches.

detail

Best of all, creamy tomato soup warms you up on a cold day. You can warm your hands. Just hold the cup or the bowl. Tomato soup warms your insides, too. For a great meal, you just can't beat tomato soup.

paragraphs

Opinion Paper Rubric

	6	5	4
Ideas	The writer's opinion is strong and clear. Specific details explain the reasons well.	The writer's opinion is clear. The reasons make sense.	The writer states an opinion. Most reasons make sense.
Organization	The writer uses a new paragraph for each idea.	Most of the writer's ideas are easy to follow.	Many of the writer's ideas are easy to follow.
Voice	The writer uses a personal "you" voice. The voice clearly speaks to the reader.	The writer generally uses a personal "you" voice and speaks to the reader.	The writer speaks to the reader some of the time.
Word Choice	Well-chosen adjectives describe the topic perfectly.	Adjectives describe the topic well.	Adjectives are used, but several could be more specific.
Sentence Fluency	Well-chosen transitions make the writing smooth and easy to follow.	Transitions are used to connect short sentences and ideas.	The same transitions are always used to connect short sentences.
Conventions	Sentences are complete. All nouns and verbs agree.	A few errors with noun and verb agreement can be fixed easily.	Several errors with noun and verb agreement confuse the reader.

+Presentation All paragraphs are indented.

What makes a good opinion paper? A rubric can help you decide. Use it to help you write. Then use it again to check your writing.

3	2	1	
The writer's opinion is unclear. The reasons are vague.	The writer's opinion is not clear. Reasons are too general or weak.	The paper does not give an opinion.	Ideas
Many of the writer's ideas are hard to follow.	Most of the writer's ideas are hard to follow.	The writing is not organized.	Organization
The writer's voice speaks to the reader and then fades.	The writer does not speak directly to the reader. The writer's voice is faint.	The writing lacks voice.	Voice
Too few or too many adjectives are used.	Many adjectives are repeated or vague. The writer's meaning is not clear.	The word choice is too general to be meaningful. The writer's meaning is not clear.	Word Choice
Transitions are not used or are used the wrong way.	Many choppy sentences make the writing hard to understand.	Sentences are incomplete.	Sentence Fluency
Many errors with noun and verb agreement make the writing hard to understand.	Serious, frequent errors with noun and verb agreement make the writing hard to understand.	Many sentences are incomplete and incorrect.	Conventions

See Appendix B for 4-, 5-, and 6-point opinion rubrics.

Using the Opinion Paper Rubric to Study the Model

Let's use the rubric to look at Mitch's opinion paper about tomato soup.

Ideas

- The writer's opinion is strong and clear.
- Specific details explain the reasons well.

Mitch's opinion is strong and clear. The very first sentence says what he thinks. Specific details help explain his reasons.

Tomato soup is the best food in the world. One reason I like it so much is that it is simple to make, since you just open a can.

Organization

- The writer uses a new paragraph for each idea.

There are three paragraphs in the paper. Each paragraph tells about one reason that Mitch likes tomato soup. Here's what the first paragraph tells about.

> One reason I like it so much is that it is simple to make, since you just open a can.

Voice

- The writer uses a personal "you" voice.
- The voice clearly speaks to the reader.

The writer uses a personal "you" voice here. I feel like I can hear Mitch talking to me.

> For a great meal, you just can't beat tomato soup.

Word Choice

- Well-chosen adjectives describe the topic perfectly.

Mitch makes his opinion clear with the adjectives he uses. What adjective does he use to describe tomato soup here?

> Best of all, creamy tomato soup warms you up on a cold day.

Sentence Fluency

- Well-chosen transitions make the writing smooth and easy to follow.

Mitch includes a lot of transitions. Look at how Mitch uses the word *Also* to show that this sentence gives more information about the paragraph's main idea.

> Also, it is perfect with most sandwiches.

Conventions

- Sentences are complete.
- All nouns and verbs agree.

All the sentences in this opinion paper are complete thoughts. The nouns and verbs in each sentence agree. Can you see how the singular noun *Tomato soup* agrees with the singular verb *warms*?

Tomato soup warms your insides, too.

+Presentation All paragraphs are indented.

My Turn!

Now it's my turn. I'm going to write an opinion paper of my own. Read on to see how I will do it.

Prewrite

Focus on Ideas

The Rubric Says The writer's opinion is strong and clear.

Writing Strategy Think about your opinions. Pick a topic about which you have a strong opinion.

Before I start writing my opinion paper, I need to choose a topic. I want to write about my favorite food, like Mitch did. First, I'll think about the foods I really like. I'll make a list of my favorites. Then, I'll choose the food that I think is the best and that has the strongest reasons.

Foods I Like	My Notes
scrambled eggs	I love eggs, but I usually eat them only for breakfast.
mashed potatoes	They taste great. They're easy to eat.
lasagna	It tastes great. It's easy to eat. It's good for you. Lasagna is the best food of all my favorites. That's my opinion. I'm going to write about lasagna!

Reflect

Tashi is going to write about lasagna. Do you think Tashi made a good choice?

Apply

Now you try! Make a list of foods you like. Then make notes about each one.

Prewrite

Focus on **Organization**

The Rubric Says The writer uses a new paragraph for each idea.

Writing Strategy Make a Network Tree to organize the reasons.

My opinion is that lasagna is the best food. The rubric says that each paragraph should have its own idea. I'll make a Network Tree to help me organize my opinion paper.

Writer's Term

Network Tree

A **Network Tree** organizes ideas. Write your opinion at the top. Write your reasons in the boxes under the topic. Then write details in the boxes under your reasons.

Topic: Lasagna Is the Best Food

Reason 1	Reason 2	Reason 3
tastes great	good for you	easy to eat
Detail	**Detail**	**Detail**
noodles and cheese	gives energy	not hard to cut

Reflect

Look at Tashi's Network Tree. Can you see how she can make one paragraph about each reason?

Apply

Using this page as a model, make your own Network Tree.

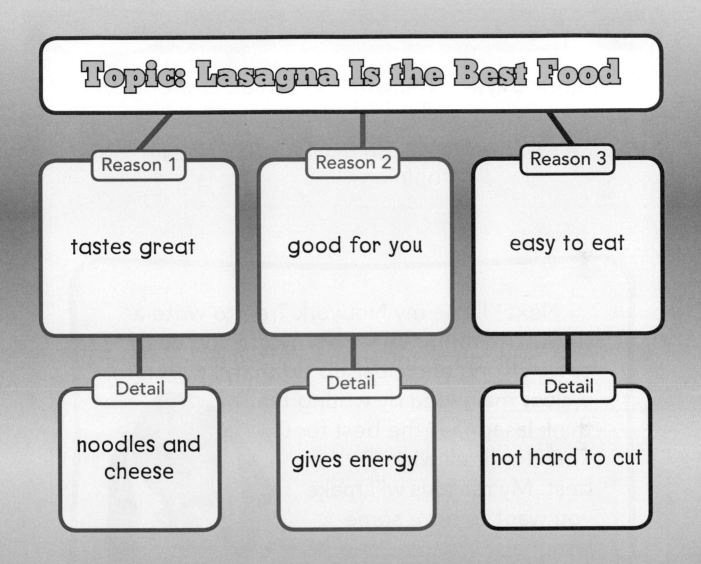

Draft

Focus on Ideas

The Rubric Says The writer's opinion is strong and clear.

Writing Strategy Include reasons that explain the opinion.

Next I'll use my Network Tree to write a draft. The rubric says that my opinion needs to be strong and clear. To do that, I will state a clear main idea by writing that I think lasagna is the best food. Then I will tell why it is the best. My reasons will make you want to have some lasagna!

Proofreading Marks

/ Make a small letter
∧ Add something
ℓ Take out something
⊙ Add a period
≡ Make a capital letter

[DRAFT]

Lasagna is the best food you can eat. One reason is that it tastes great. That's because it have noodles and cheese. has tomato sauce, too. Another reason is that lasagna is easy to eat. It isn't hard to cut. It isn't hard to chew, either. It doesn't stick to your teeth.

Lasagna is the best food because it is good for you, too. Lasagna fills you up and gives you energy. Lasagna!

clear opinion

Reflect

Did Tashi follow the rubric? How does Tashi make her opinion clear?

Apply

Look at your notes and your Network Tree. Start writing your draft.

Revise

Focus on **Ideas**

The Rubric Says	Specific details explain the reasons well.
Writing Strategy	Add details that explain the reasons.

Next I need to revise. That means changing some things to make my opinion paper even better. The rubric says that I should include specific details to explain my reasons well. I will reread my paper to see if I have explained my reasons well enough. If not, I'll add more details.

[DRAFT]

Another reason is that lasagna is easy to eat. It isn't hard to cut. It isn't hard to chew, either. It doesn't stick to your teeth.

Lasagna is the best food because it is good for you, too. The cheese helps build your bones. The sauce has vitamins. Lasagna fills you up and gives you energy. Lasagna!

added details

Reflect

Did Tashi use specific details? Do the details explain her reasons well?

Apply

Now look at your draft. Find places where you can add details.

Revise

Focus on Organization

The Rubric Says The writer uses a new paragraph for each idea.

Writing Strategy Make sure each paragraph is about one idea.

The rubric says that each idea should have its own paragraph. I will check each paragraph to be sure it talks about just one idea. If two ideas are in the paragraph, I will make a new paragraph about one of the ideas by indenting the first line.

[DRAFT]

Lasagna is the best food you can eat. One reason is that it tastes great. That's because it have noodles and cheese. has tomato sauce, too.

Another reason is that lasagna is easy to eat. It isn't hard to cut. It isn't hard to chew, either. It doesn't stick to your teeth.

indented paragraph

Reflect

Did Tashi talk about one idea in each paragraph? What might happen if Tashi put more than one idea in a paragraph?

Apply

Look at your draft. Do the sentences in each paragraph belong together? Can you make a new paragraph when you find a new idea?

Edit

Focus on Conventions

The Rubric Says Sentences are complete. All nouns and verbs agree.

Writing Strategy Check each sentence carefully.

Next I'll edit my paper. I will check every word and fix any mistakes I find. The rubric says that sentences should be complete. I'll need to check that every sentence has a subject and a predicate. The rubric also says that all nouns and verbs should agree. If I find any that don't, I'll fix them.

Writer's Term

Subject and Predicate

The **subject** of a sentence has a noun. It tells **who** or **what**. The **predicate** tells what action the subject takes or tells about the subject.

[DRAFT]

made noun and verb agree

added subject

One reason is that it tastes great. That's because it ~~have~~ has soft noodles and melted cheese. Lasagna has yummy tomato sauce, too.

Another reason is that lasagna is easy to eat, since ~~I~~t isn't hard to cut. It isn't hard to chew, either. Also, ~~I~~t doesn't stick to your teeth.

Lasagna is the best food because it is good for you, too. The cheese helps build your bones. The sauce has vitamins. Lasagna fills you up and gives you energy. You should try it! Lasagna is the best food of all!

added predicate

Reflect

Are Tashi's sentences complete? Do all of her nouns and verbs agree?

Apply

Make sure every sentence in your draft is complete. Also make sure nouns and verbs agree. See the next two pages for more practice.

Subjects and Predicates

Know the Rule

A complete sentence must have a **subject** and a **predicate**.

Practice the Rule

Number a sheet of paper 1–8. Write the sentences. Circle the subject. Underline the predicate.

1. My friend Priya is from India.
2. Her mom makes spicy food to eat.
3. The spicy food is called curry.
4. It has rice and vegetables.
5. Their family eats curry with warm bread.
6. The bread is called naan.
7. Naan with garlic tastes great!
8. I enjoy trying new foods.

Subject-Verb Agreement

Know the Rule

The **subject** and its **verb** must agree in number.
Example: My **friends like** Indian food.

Collective nouns tell about more than one person.
But they take a singular verb.
Example: My **family likes** Indian food.

Practice the Rule

Number a separate sheet of paper 1–6. Write **yes** if the underlined noun and verb agree. Write **no** and the correct verb if they do not agree.

1. I love pizza.
2. The cheese is the best part.
3. My favorite toppings is mushrooms and onions.
4. My friend like pepperoni.
5. We get half and half when we order together.
6. Sometimes we makes our own pizza.

Publish

+Presentation

Publishing Strategy Post the paper on the class bulletin board.

Presentation Strategy Indent every paragraph.

I finished my paper! Now I'll make a final copy with neat handwriting or careful word processing. I will make sure that my paragraphs are indented. Later I'll post my paper on our classroom bulletin board. I will use this checklist to publish my paper. You can use it to check your draft, too.

My Final Checklist

Did I —

✔ fix all of the mistakes?

✔ make sure every sentence has a subject and a predicate?

✔ indent each paragraph?

FINAL DRAFT

The Best Food

by Tashi

Lasagna is the best food you can eat. One reason is that it tastes great. That's because it has soft noodles and melted cheese. Lasagna has yummy tomato sauce, too.

Another reason is that lasagna is easy to eat, since it isn't hard to cut. It isn't hard to chew, either. Also, it doesn't stick to your teeth.

Lasagna is the best food because it is good for you, too. The cheese helps build your bones. The sauce has vitamins. Lasagna fills you up and gives you energy. You should try it. Lasagna is the best food of all!

Reflect

Did Tashi follow the rubric? Use the rubric to check your final draft, too.

Parts of a Response to Literature

A response to literature is a way of sharing what I have read. In it, I can tell what I think about the book. I will write a book report. If the book is good, my response might make you want to read it, too.

Opinion

An opinion is what I think or believe. You might agree with my opinion. Or you might have your own opinion.

Reasons

Reasons explain something. They can be used to explain or support an opinion.

Conclusion

A conclusion is an ending. It is the closing part. A conclusion often states the opinion over again.

Reasons for Writing a Response to Literature

Here are some reasons to write a response to literature.

To inform
I can tell others what a book is about. They can learn about the book by reading my response.

To entertain
Most stories are fun to read. I can write about the best parts. Readers will enjoy my response. It will entertain them.

To convince
My response might make others want to read the book.

Linking Opinion Writing Traits to a Response to Literature

In this chapter, you will give an opinion about a book you have read. This type of writing is called a response to literature. Tashi will guide you through the stages of the writing process. She will also show you some writing strategies that are linked to the Opinion Writing Traits below.

Opinion Writing Traits

Ideas	• a clearly stated opinion • reasons that support the opinion
Organization	• a strong introduction, body, and conclusion • transitions that connect opinion and reasons
Voice	• a voice and tone that are perfect for the piece of writing
Word Choice	• strong words that convince the reader
Sentence Fluency	• varied sentences
Conventions	• no or few errors in spelling, punctuation, and capitalization

Let's read this model of a response to literature. We can use the rubric on the next two pages to check his writing.

Response to Literature **MODEL**

Henry and Mudge and the Bedtime Thumps
by Cynthia Rylant
reviewed by Felix

In this book, Henry and his parents and his dog, Mudge, go to visit his grandmother. I like this book because Henry is like me. We both like dogs.

opinion

How do I know Henry likes dogs? Henry worries about Mudge. He does not want Mudge to sleep outside. Henry cannot sleep at night without Mudge.

Mudge is naughty, and he has to go outside. He even has to sleep outside. Henry cannot sleep. He hears thumps, but Mudge is not there to protect him. So Henry finds Mudge, and they sleep together on the porch.

reasons

Henry is happy when Mudge is happy. I am happy when my dog is happy. If you like dogs, you will like this book, too.

conclusion

Response to Literature Rubric

	6	5	4
Ideas	The opinion is clearly stated and well supported by reasons.	The opinion is clearly stated and supported by reasons.	The opinion is stated. A couple of reasons are given.
Organization	The writer presents details in perfect order. The conclusion wraps up the writing.	One detail is out of order. There is a conclusion.	Most details are in order. There is a conclusion.
Voice	The writer uses a personal "I" voice and clearly speaks to the reader.	The writer generally uses a personal "I" voice and speaks to the reader.	The writer speaks to the reader some of the time.
Word Choice	Excellent word choice allows the reader to understand the writer's reasons.	Specific words help the reader understand all the reasons.	Most of the words help the reader understand the reasons.
Sentence Fluency	Sentences of different lengths make the writing easy and fun to read.	Most of the sentences are varied and the writing is easy to read.	Some sentences are the same length. The writing is choppy.
Conventions	Conjunctions and compound sentences are used correctly.	A few errors with conjunctions and compound sentences can be easily corrected.	Some errors with conjunctions and compound sentences confuse the reader.

+Presentation Use good spacing between words and lines.

What makes a good response to literature? A rubric can help you decide. Use it to help you write. Then use it again to check your writing.

3	2	1	
The opinion is unclear. The reasons do not support a single opinion.	No opinion is stated.	It is not clear what the response is about.	Ideas
The details are confusing. There is no conclusion.	The details are incomplete. Some may be missing.	The details do not help explain a topic.	Organization
The writer's voice speaks to the reader and then fades.	The writer does not speak directly to the reader. The writer's voice is faint.	The writing lacks voice.	Voice
Many words are repeated or vague. The writer's meaning is not clear.	The word choice is too general to be meaningful. The writer's meaning is not clear.	The words do not express an opinion.	Word Choice
Many sentences are the same length and make the writing choppy to read.	Sentences are usually the same length and the reader must work to read them.	Sentences are too long, lack variety, or are incomplete and the writing is hard to follow.	Sentence Fluency
Many errors with conjunctions and compound sentences make the reader struggle to understand.	Numerous errors with conjunctions and compound sentences confuse the reader.	Serious, frequent errors make the writing hard to understand.	Conventions

See Appendix B for 4-, 5-, and 6-point descriptive rubrics.

Using the Rubric to Study the Model

Response to Literature

Let's use the rubric to check Felix's response to literature about the book, *Henry and Mudge and the Bedtime Thumps.*

Ideas

- The opinion is clearly stated and well supported by reasons.

Felix tells why he likes the book. He says Henry is like him. They both like dogs. Then Felix lists the reasons from the book that show him that Henry likes dogs.

I like this book because Henry is like me. We both like dogs.

How do I know Henry likes dogs? Henry worries about Mudge. He does not want Mudge to sleep outside. Henry cannot sleep at night without Mudge.

Organization

- The writer presents details in perfect order. The conclusion wraps up the writing.

When Felix tells what happens at Grandmother's house, he tells the details in an order that makes sense. He tells the details in the order they happened. Then Felix ends with a conclusion.

> Henry cannot sleep. He hears thumps, but Mudge is not there to protect him. So Henry finds Mudge, and they sleep together on the porch.
>
> Henry is happy when Mudge is happy. I am happy when my dog is happy.

Voice

- The writer uses a personal "I" voice and clearly speaks to the reader.

Voice is the way writing sounds. Using *I*, *me*, and *we* makes the response warm and friendly. It is as if Felix is talking with his readers. I can also tell that Felix really likes the book.

> I like this book because Henry is like me. We both like dogs.
>
> How do I know Henry likes dogs?

Word Choice

- Excellent word choice allows the reader to understand the writer's reasons.

Specific words are better than general words. Felix says Henry hears *thumps*, not *noises*. He uses the word *protect*, which is stronger than *help* or *watch*.

> He hears thumps, but Mudge is not there to protect him.

Sentence Fluency

- Sentences of different lengths make the writing easy and fun to read.

Some sentences are long. Other sentences are short. One has only three words. Felix did a good job of writing sentences of different lengths.

> Mudge is naughty, and he has to go outside. He even has to sleep outside. Henry cannot sleep.

Conventions

- Conjunctions and compound sentences are used correctly.

A compound sentence is made from two sentences joined together. The two sentences Felix uses are *Mudge is naughty* and *He has to go outside*. The sentences are joined together with a comma and the conjunction *and. And* tells me that these ideas are related.

Mudge is naughty, and he has to go outside.

Presentation Use good spacing between words and lines.

My Turn!

Now it's my turn. I'm going to write my own response to literature. Read on to see how I will do it.

Prewrite

Focus on **Ideas**

The Rubric Says The opinion is clearly stated and well supported by reasons.

Writing Strategy Take notes for the reasons.

Before I begin writing, I need to choose a book and read it. I will form an opinion about the book. Then I can take notes by writing down the reasons for my opinion. I will use these notes when I write my book report.

Book: *Amelia Bedelia* **by Peggy Parish**

Opinion:

I liked this book. Anyone would like it. It is a funny book.

Reasons:

1. To change the towels, Amelia cuts them so they have a different shape.
2. To dust the furniture, she puts dusting powder on it.
3. To draw the drapes, she draws a picture of them.

Reflect

Read Tashi's notes. Does she have enough reasons to support her opinion that the book is funny?

Apply

Decide what book to write about. Then write your opinion and some reasons to support it.

Prewrite

Focus on **Organization**

The Rubric Says The writer presents details in perfect order. The conclusion wraps up the writing.

Writing Strategy Make a Sequence Chart to organize the book report.

An organizer can help me plan my book report. When I tell about the story, I will be sure to put all the details in order. I will put them in the order they happened. I can use a Sequence Chart to help me decide what to write at the beginning, middle, and end of my report.

Writer's Term

Sequence Chart

A **Sequence Chart** helps me remember what I will write at the beginning, in the middle, and at the end of my book report.

Book Report: *Amelia Bedelia* by Peggy Parish

Beginning	Opinion
Middle	Reasons (in this order): towels furniture drapes
End	Conclusion

Reflect

Look at Tashi's Sequence Chart. How does it show what she will write about at the beginning, middle, and end of her book report?

Apply

Make your own Sequence Chart. Use this page as a model.

Draft

Focus on Organization

The Rubric Says The writer presents details in perfect order.

Writing Strategy Put the opinion first and the reasons in the middle.

Next I will use my Sequence Chart to start my draft. First, I will state my opinion. This way the reader knows what to expect. Then, I will give reasons for my opinion. Because the book has so many funny things, I may not have room to tell all of them. I can pick the best ones. Finally, I will write the conclusion. It is the last thing I will write.

Before I publish my writing, I will look for spelling, capitalization, or punctuation mistakes and fix them.

Proofreading Marks

- / Make a small letter
- ∧ Add something
- Take out something
- ⊙ Add a period
- ≡ Make a capital letter

[DRAFT]

Amelia Bedelia by Peggy Parish

Book Report by Tashi

I loved this book. We think you will like it, too, because it is funny. In it, Amelia does some funny things. She is supposed to clean the house, and she doesn't.

clear opinion

To change the towels, Amelia cuts them so they have a different shape. To dust the furniture, she puts dusting powder on it. To draw the drapes, Amelia draws a picture of them.

reasons

Reflect

Read the beginning of Tashi's draft. What is Tashi's opinion?

Apply

Write your first draft. Start by stating your opinion. Then give reasons.

Revise

Focus on Voice

The Rubric Says The writer uses a personal "I" voice and clearly speaks to the reader.

Writing Strategy Try to sound like yourself.

Voice is the way writing sounds. A report on rocks needs a serious voice. A report about telling jokes needs a fun voice.

The purpose of my book report is to convince others to read the book. Using *I* and *me* in my writing makes the readers feel like a friend is speaking to them. Using *I* and a polite tone might convince my readers to read this book.

Writer's Term

Voice

Voice is the way writing sounds. A good voice sounds as if the writer were talking. Using **I** and **me** makes the writer's voice sound very personal.

[DRAFT]

used a personal voice.

Amelia Bedelia by Peggy Parish

Book Report by Tashi

I loved this book. I ~~We~~ think you will like it, too, because it is funny. In it, Amelia does some funny things. She is supposed to clean the house, and she doesn't.

To change the towels, Amelia cuts them so they have a different shape. To dust the furniture, she puts dusting powder on it. To draw the drapes, Amelia draws a picture of them.

Reflect

Does Tashi's revision make sense? Does her writing voice sound better?

Apply

Read your draft aloud. Listen for the voice in your writing. Make changes so that your writing sounds more personal.

Revise

Focus on Word Choice

The Rubric Says Excellent word choice allows the reader to understand the writer's reasons.

Writing Strategy Use specific words.

Specific words help readers more than general or vague words. I will be sure to use specific words wherever I can.

In my book report, I talk about Amelia. This might be confusing. In a book report, words like *character, author,* and *title* tell the readers exactly which part of the book I am talking about. I could say that Amelia is a character in the book. That will be clearer.

[DRAFT]

Amelia Bedelia by Peggy Parish
Book Report by Tashi

I loved this book. I ~~We~~ think you will like it, too, because it is funny. In it, a character named Amelia does some funny things. She is supposed to clean the house, and she doesn't.

added a specific word

Reflect

Did Tashi follow the rubric? How does identifying Amelia as a character make the meaning more clear and specific?

Apply

Look at your draft. Check to see if you have written any parts that are vague or too general. Change them to make them more specific.

Edit

Focus on Conventions

The Rubric Says Conjunctions and compound sentences are used correctly.

Writing Strategy Use conjunctions correctly.

The next thing I will do is correct mistakes in spelling and punctuation. The rubric also says to check the conjunctions. Conjunctions can join two words together. They also can join two related sentences to make a compound sentence.

Each conjunction has a different meaning. I should be sure that I have used the correct one. I found a place where I used *and*. The conjunction *but* makes the sentence clearer. Do you agree?

Writer's Term

Conjunctions

Conjunctions are words that connect words or sentences. The words **and, but**, and **or** are conjunctions.

[DRAFT]

Amelia Bedelia by Peggy Parish
Book Report by Tashi

I loved this book. I ~~We~~ think you will like it, too, because it is funny. In it, a character named Amelia does some funny things. She is supposed to clean the house, but ~~and~~ she does everything wrong ~~doesn't~~.

To change the towels, Amelia cuts them so they have a different shape.

fixed a conjunction

Reflect

Does the word *but* make the meaning clearer?

Apply

Now check your draft. Make sure you have used conjunctions correctly. For more practice with conjunctions, turn to the next page.

Conjunctions

Know the Rule

The words *and, or,* and *but* can join two words in a sentence. They are called **conjunctions**.

Examples:

The dress is trimmed with lace **and** ribbons.
Would you like eggs **or** pancakes for breakfast?
I put nuts **but** not raisins on my cereal.

Practice the Rule

Number a separate sheet of paper 1–6. Write **and, or,** or **but** to complete each sentence.

1. Both Sandy ____ Jill have read that book.
2. Was it Denny ____ Tom who won the race?
3. Tina likes to play softball ____ not basketball.
4. I got the red shoes ____ not the black shoes.
5. Do you want to paint ____ draw with crayons?
6. Those backpacks belong to Carlo ____ Julian.

Compound Sentences

Know the Rule

And, or, and *but* can also join two short sentences. The new sentence is called a **compound sentence**.

Example: Some trees are tall, **but** other trees are short.

Practice the Rule

Number a separate sheet of paper 1–8. Write the conjunction (**and, but, or**) that joins the two sentences together.

1. Ted can ride his bike, ____ he can go swimming.
2. Tigers can run, ____ they cannot fly.
3. Hong Li likes grapes, ____ she does not like bananas.
4. One team wears red, ____ the other team wears green.
5. Seth threw the ball, ____ Kim caught it.
6. Franklin can have a salad, ____ he can eat tacos for lunch.
7. Chapter books are here, ____ poetry is over there.
8. Lisa must put on her coat, ____ she will get cold.

Publish

+Presentation

Publishing Strategy Read the book report to the class.

Presentation Strategy Check the spacing.

I finished my book report! Next I will make a neat final copy using good spacing between words and lines. This way, I can practice reading it aloud easily. Then I will be ready to read it to the class. Maybe our teacher will let us record our book reports!

My Final Checklist

Did I —

- ✔ correct any mistakes?
- ✔ use my best handwriting?
- ✔ read with my best voice?

FINAL DRAFT

Amelia Bedelia by Peggy Parish
Book Report by Tashi

I loved this book. I think you will like it, too, because it is funny. In it, a character named Amelia does some funny things. She is supposed to clean the house, but she does everything wrong.

To change the towels, Amelia cuts them so they have a different shape. To dust the furniture, she puts dusting powder on it. To draw the drapes, Amelia draws a picture of them.

This book is funny, and you will like it. Read this book. You will get a good laugh!

Reflect

How did Tashi do? Use the rubric to check your final draft.

Parts of an Opinion Speech

An opinion speech is a talk that I give when I want to tell people what I think. My speech might be about something at school or in my community.

Opinion

To give my opinion, I'll tell what I think about my topic. I'll tell my opinion at the beginning of the speech.

Reasons

I'll give reasons to explain and support my opinion. Reasons tell facts or tell the way I feel.

Paragraphs

A paragraph is a group of sentences. I will write a paragraph for each of my reasons.

Facts

A fact is something that can be proved. Facts will help to convince the reader.

Conclusion

The conclusion is at the end of the paper. It's where I tell my opinion again and end my speech.

Reasons for Writing an Opinion Speech

Here are some reasons to write an opinion speech.

To share
I like to share ideas with my friends and family. If I write my ideas down on paper, it's easier to remember what I want to say when I give a speech to them.

To convince
When I wanted a bicycle, I wrote an opinion speech about it for my parents. They decided that if I could help pay for it, I could get one!

To help
I can help make my school or community a nicer place if I try to change things for the better. Giving an opinion speech can make a difference.

Linking Opinion Writing Traits to an Opinion Speech

In this chapter, you will write about what you think or feel strongly about. This type of writing is called an opinion speech. Tashi will guide you through the stages of the writing process. She will also show you some writing strategies that are linked to the Opinion Writing Traits below.

Opinion Writing Traits

Ideas	• a clearly stated opinion • reasons that support the opinion
Organization	• a strong introduction, body, and conclusion • transitions that connect opinions and reasons
Voice	• a voice and tone that are perfect for the piece of writing
Word Choice	• strong words that convince the reader
Sentence Fluency	• varied sentences
Conventions	• no or few errors in spelling, punctuation, and capitalization

Let's look at this model of an opinion speech. Lisa thinks her school library needs more computers. We can use the rubric to check her writing.

Opinion Speech MODEL

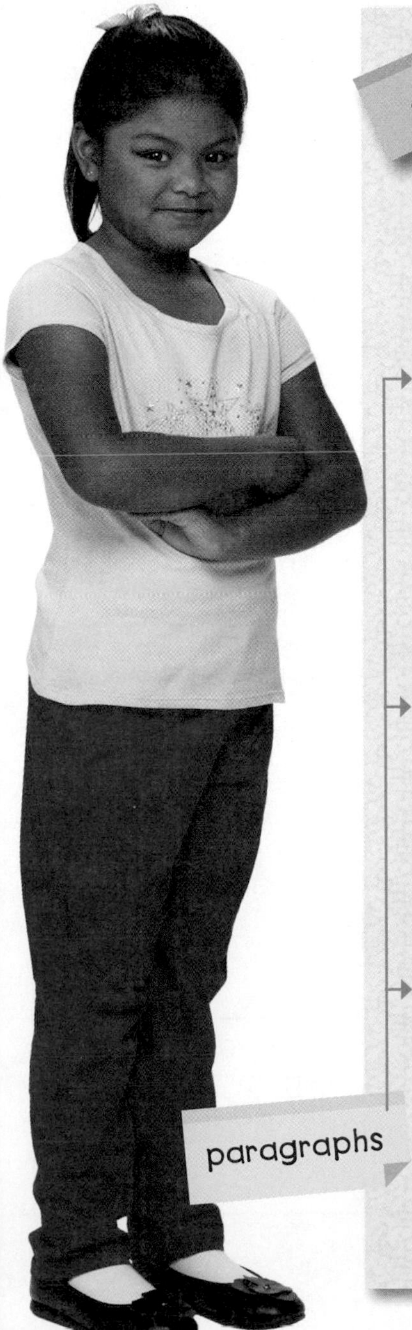

opinion

Computers in Our Library

by Lisa Lowell

We need more computers in our library. With more computers, we could spend more time writing on the computer. Now each student can use a computer for only ten minutes at a time. That is not enough!

reason

With more computers, we could use the Internet more. Right now, we can't look up things when we need to. Sometimes we have to wait for hours or even days.

fact

With more computers, we could learn better computer skills. Some of us don't know how to use a search engine or how to find the right keys on the keyboard. We could learn these things if we had more computers. More computers will help us all!

conclusion

paragraphs

Opinion Speech Rubric

	6	5	4
Ideas	The writer's opinion is strong and clear. Facts convince the reader.	The writer's opinion is clear. The speech has facts.	The writer states an opinion. Some facts are weak.
Organization	Each paragraph supports one reason. The conclusion wraps up the writing.	One paragraph supports more than one reason. There is a conclusion.	Two paragraphs support more than one reason. There is a conclusion.
Voice	The writer uses *we* to include and convince the reader.	The writer includes the reader most of the time.	The writer starts out using *we* but does not continue to the end.
Word Choice	Well-chosen adjectives describe the topic perfectly.	Adjectives describe the topic well.	Adjectives are used, but several could be more specific.
Sentence Fluency	Each sentence makes a point. Similar sentences emphasize a point.	Most of the sentences are clear and make a point.	Some sentences are clear and make a point.
Conventions	Irregular verbs are used and spelled correctly.	A few errors with irregular verbs can be easily corrected.	Some errors with irregular verbs confuse the reader.

+Presentation The speech is neat and legible.

A rubric can help you decide if a piece of writing needs more work. Use it when you write. Then use it again to check your writing.

3	2	1	
The writer's opinion is unclear. Not all the facts support the opinion.	The writer's opinion is not clear. Some facts are wrong.	The paper does not give an opinion.	Ideas
The same reason is explained in two paragraphs. The conclusion is weak.	The paragraphs are not clear. There is no conclusion.	The speech is not organized into paragraphs.	Organization
The writer's use of *we* goes back and forth.	The writer does not include the reader.	The writer does not sound prepared.	Voice
Too few or too many adjectives are used.	Many adjectives are repeated or vague. The writer's meaning is not clear.	The word choice is too general to be meaningful. The writer's meaning is not clear.	Word Choice
Too many sentences are similar, which makes the writing confusing.	Many sentences do not have a point and are not clear.	Sentences are incomplete.	Sentence Fluency
Many errors with irregular verbs make the reader struggle to understand.	Numerous errors with irregular verbs confuse the reader.	Serious, frequent errors make the writing hard to understand.	Conventions

See Appendix B for 4-, 5-, and 6-point opinion rubrics.

Using the Opinion Speech Rubric to Study the Model

Let's use the rubric to check Lisa's speech about computers for her school library.

Ideas

- The writer's opinion is strong and clear.
- Facts convince the reader.

Lisa feels strongly about her opinion. She writes only about why the school needs more computers in the library. The facts she uses to support her opinion are very convincing!

> Sometimes we have to wait for hours or even days.

Organization

- Each paragraph supports one reason.
- The conclusion wraps up the writing.

Every paragraph gives a different reason. The conclusion wraps all Lisa's ideas together.

> More computers will help us all!

Voice

- The writer uses *we* to include and convince the reader.

Lisa wants to convince her readers to agree with her. She uses *we* to draw readers in and get them on her side.

> Right now, we can't look up things when we need to.

Word Choice

- Well-chosen adjectives describe the topic perfectly.

Lisa uses the adjective *better* to describe one of the reasons supporting her opinion.

> With more computers, we could learn better computer skills.

Sentence Fluency

- Each sentence makes a point.
- Similar sentences emphasize a point.

Each of Lisa's sentences make a point. She uses similar sentences to make her message stronger. Look at how these three sentences start the same way. They really make the point that Lisa wants more computers.

> With more computers, we could spend more time writing on the computer.
>
> With more computers, we could use the Internet more.
>
> With more computers, we could learn better computer skills.

Conventions

- Irregular verbs are used and spelled correctly.

Lisa knows her verbs well. She has spelled them all correctly, even the irregular verbs. She knows that the past tense of *has* is *had.*

We could learn these things if we had more computers. More computers will help us all!

Presentation The speech is neat and legible.

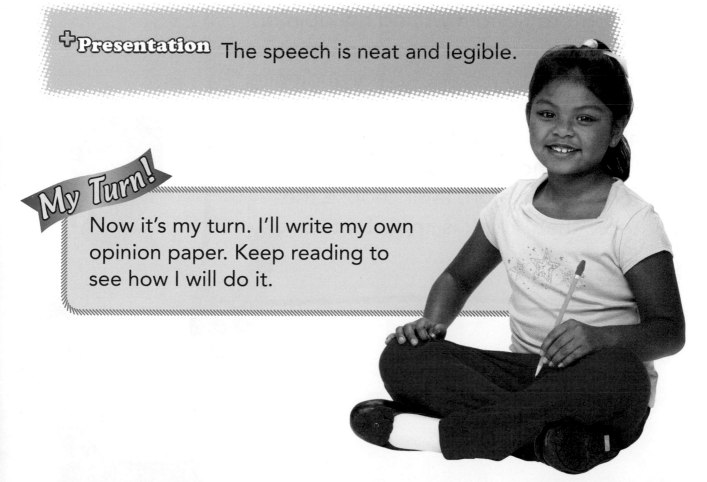

My Turn!

Now it's my turn. I'll write my own opinion paper. Keep reading to see how I will do it.

Prewrite

Focus on Ideas

The Rubric Says The writer's opinion is strong and clear.

Writing Strategy Think about your opinions on different topics. Write some reasons for your opinions. Then choose the best topic.

Before I begin writing my opinion speech, I need to pick a topic that is important to me and to my audience. First, I will write down some topics and my opinions about them. Then, I'll make notes about my reasons for each opinion. I will choose the topic that I think is important to the most people.

My Topics	My Notes
school bus	• My opinion: It should have seat belts. • My reason: It would be safer. • My thoughts: I don't have enough facts about this topic. I won't use this one.
playground	• My opinion: We should fix it up! • My reasons: The swings are in bad shape. The slide shakes. The basketball court isn't safe. • My thoughts: I have a lot of facts about this topic. It is also very important to my friends. They'll be my audience. I'll use this one.

Reflect

Do you think Tashi picked a topic she feels strongly about? Will it be important to her audience?

Apply

Make a list of topics for your own opinion speech. Make notes about each one.

Prewrite

Focus on **Organization**

The Rubric Says Each paragraph supports one reason.

Writing Strategy Make an Opinion Chart to organize the reasons.

I have a whole bunch of reasons for my opinion. The rubric says each paragraph should support one reason. I'll make an Opinion Chart to organize my reasons. I'll write my topic at the top of the chart. Then I'll put one reason in each box on the left. On the right, I'll write a fact to support each reason. I'll use the chart to write my speech.

Writer's Term

Opinion Chart

An **Opinion Chart** helps to organize an opinion paper or speech. The reasons are listed on one side. Facts about the reasons are listed on the other side.

Graphic Organizer: Opinion Chart

Topic: We Should Fix Our Playground	
Reasons	**Facts**
• swings in bad shape	• chains rusty
• slide shakes	• old and wobbly
• basketball court isn't safe	• cracks in pavement

Reflect

Do you think Tashi can make a paragraph from each of her reasons? Will she need to add more details?

Apply

Now you try! Make an Opinion Chart to organize the reasons and facts for your opinion speech.

Draft

Focus on Voice

The Rubric Says The writer uses *we* to include and convince the reader.

Writing Strategy Use *we* to make the reader feel part of the writing.

I'm writing this speech because I want people to do something about my ideas. By using the word *we*, I include my readers in my thoughts. I hope to convince them to agree with me. I'll use *we* to make it sound like my readers and I will work together to make a difference!

Proofreading Marks

/ Make a small letter
∧ Add something
ℓ Take out something
⊙ Add a period
≡ Make a capital letter

[DRAFT]

used we

We should fix up our playground. One reason is that the swings are in bad shape. The chains are rusty. The swings look terrible.

The second reason we should fix up our playground is that the slide is old and wobbly. It shakes when you climb it. Nobody wants to use it.

The third reason is that there are cracks in the basketball court. It is dangerous! You should make our playground a safer place!

Reflect

Did Tashi follow the rubric? Did she draw in her reader by using *we*?

Apply

Now you try it. Look at your topic, notes, and your Opinion Chart. Start writing!

Revise

Focus on Word Choice

The Rubric Says	Well-chosen adjectives describe the topic perfectly.
Writing Strategy	Use adjectives that will convince the reader to agree with the opinion.

Choosing adjectives carefully will help to make my points stronger. I will use adjectives to help my readers understand my point. Adjectives will help me describe how bad things are on the playground so I can win over my readers!

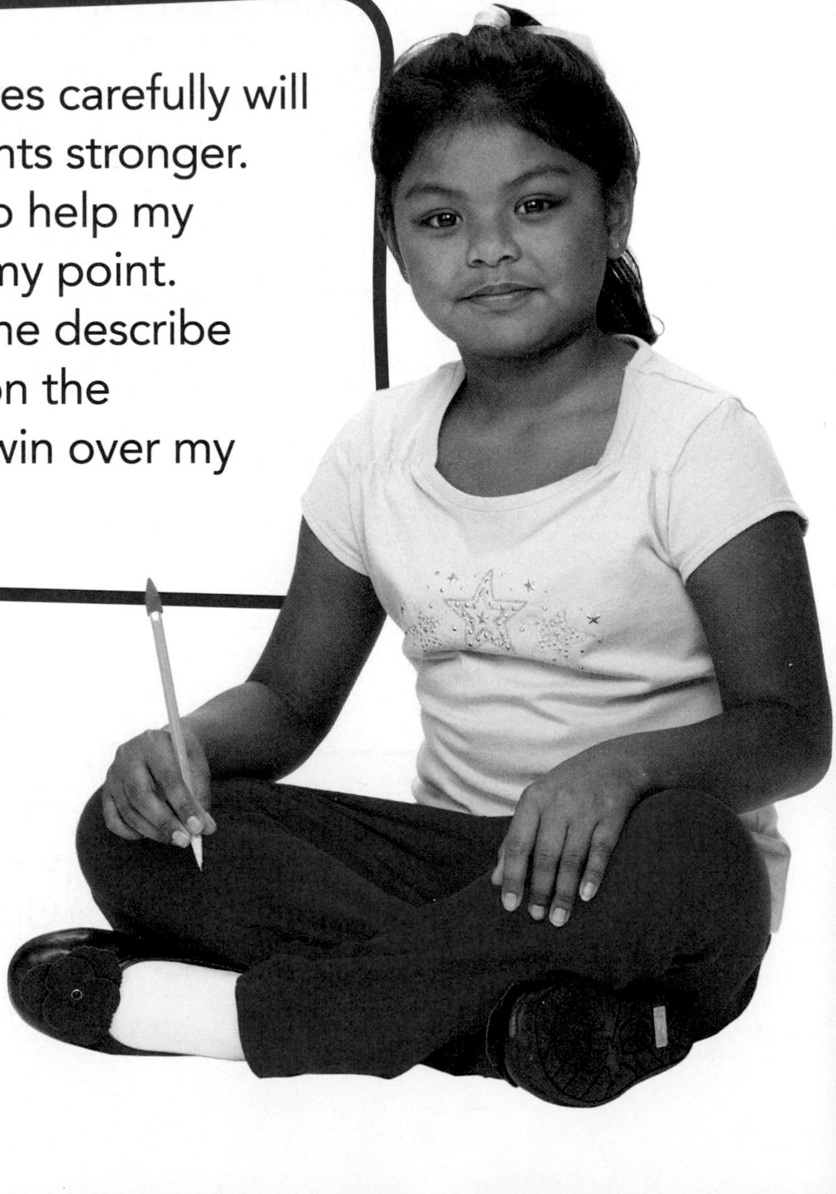

[DRAFT]

We should fix up our playground. One reason is that the swings are in bad shape. The squeaky chains are rusty. The swings look terrible.

The second reason we should fix up our playground is that the slide is old and wobbly. It shakes when you climb it. Nobody wants to use it.

The third reason is that there are deep cracks in the basketball court. It is dangerous! You should make our playground a safer place!

added adjectives

Reflect

Look at how Tashi added adjectives. Do you see how the words add to her description?

Apply

Now look at your draft. Can you add any adjectives to improve your description?

Revise

Focus on **Sentence Fluency**

The Rubric Says	Each sentence makes a point. Similar sentences emphasize a point.
Writing Strategy	Make some of the sentences sound similar.

I will read my speech again to make sure I'm doing everything the rubric says. It says that my speech will be stronger if some of my sentences sound similar. I remember how Lisa did that in her opinion speech. I'll make my reasons sound similar. That will really help make my point.

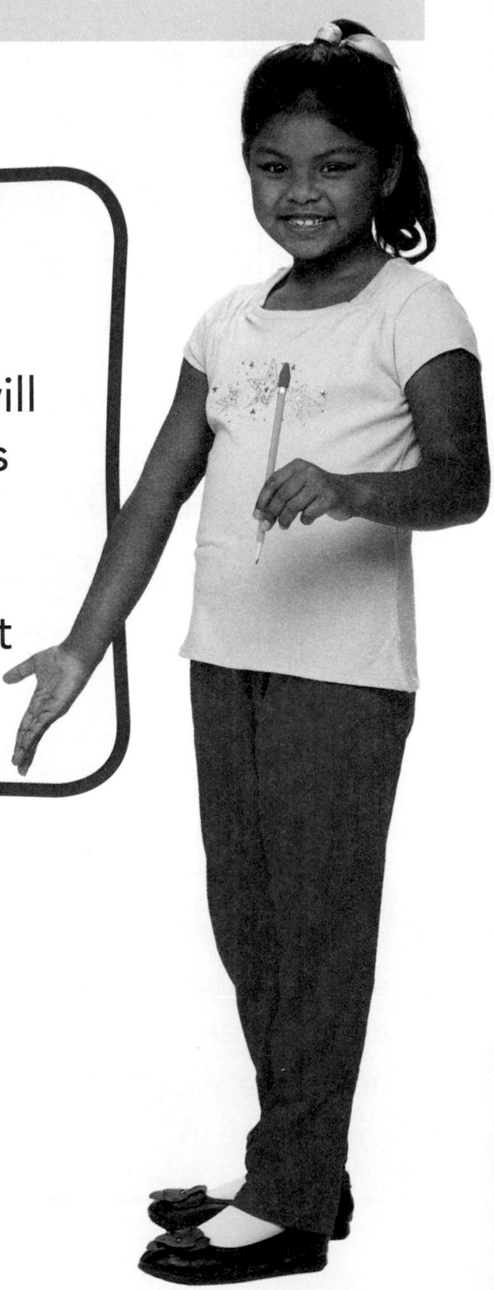

[DRAFT]

made some sentences similar

The second reason we should fix up our playground is that the slide is old and wobbly. It shakes when you climb it. Nobody wants to use it.

The third reason we should fix up our playground is that there are deep cracks in the basketball court. It is dangerous! You should make our playground a safer place!

Reflect

Do you see how Tashi made some sentences similar? How does doing that help her point?

Apply

Look at your draft. Are there any sentences that could sound similar?

Edit

Focus on Conventions

The Rubric Says Irregular verbs are used and spelled correctly.

Writing Strategy Check the verbs.

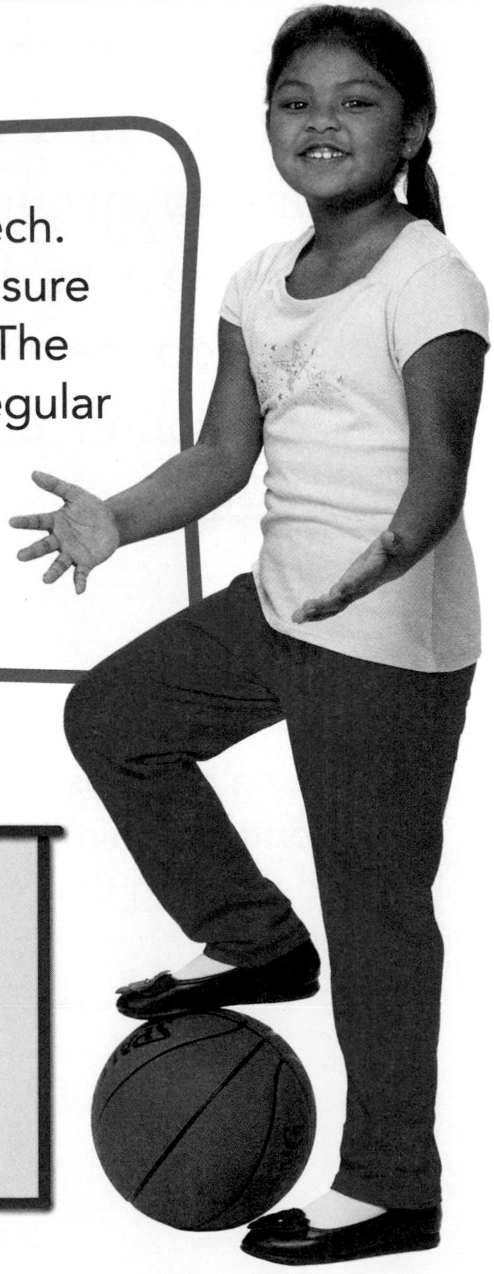

Now I'm ready to edit my speech. I will check my spelling and make sure that my sentences are complete. The rubric says I also need to spell irregular verbs correctly. I'll check my sentences to see if I need to fix any irregular verbs.

Writer's Term

Irregular Verbs

Irregular verbs form the past tense in different ways. They do not end in **-ed**. Here are some irregular verbs: **come/came, do/did, swim/swam.**

[DRAFT]

The second reason we should fix up our playground is that the slide is old and wobbly. It shakes when you climb it. Nobody wants to use it.

The third reason we should fix up our playground is that there are deep cracks in the basketball court. It is dangerous! Once someone fell ~~fall~~ down. Let's ~~You should~~ make our playground a safer place today!

fixed irregular verb

Reflect

Look at how Tashi fixed an irregular verb. Do you see how it makes the meaning more clear?

Apply

Now check your draft of your own opinion speech. Make sure you spelled all irregular verb forms correctly. For more practice with irregular verbs, turn to the next page.

Irregular Verbs

Know the Rule

Many verbs form the past tense by adding *-ed*.
Irregular verbs do not add *-ed*.

Present	go	hide	run	sit	tell	write
Past	went	hid	ran	sat	told	wrote

Practice the Rule

Number a sheet of paper 1–8. Write the form of the verb that completes the sentence.

1. My friend José (go/went) outside for recess.
2. He (sit/sat) on the swings.
3. He (write/wrote) on the pavement with chalk.
4. José (hide/hid) behind the slide during hide-and-seek.
5. He (run/ran) across the yard during a game of tag.
6. He (tell/told) Maria that she was "it."
7. Maria (run/ran) after José.
8. Maria (tell/told) José that he was "it!"

More Irregular Verbs

Know the Rule

Here are some more **irregular verbs**.

Present	be	begin	eat	forget	have	keep
Past	was	began	ate	forgot	had	kept

Practice the Rule

Number a sheet of paper 1–8. Write the form of the verb that completes the sentence.

1. Sara (eat/ate) her snack.
2. Then it (be/was) time for recess.
3. She (forget/forgot) her jump rope.
4. Her friend Julie (have/had) an extra rope for her.
5. Sara (begin/began) to jump rope.
6. She (forget/forgot) the words to a jump-rope rhyme.
7. Sara (keep/kept) the rope for all of recess.
8. Soon it (be/was) time to go inside.

Publish

+Presentation

Publishing Strategy Give the speech to the class.

Presentation Strategy Use neat handwriting or word processing.

I finished my speech! Now I'll make a neat final copy. This will help me when I read it in front of the class. If my copy is too messy, I might make mistakes. I will need to speak loudly, clearly, and not too fast for my audience. I will use this checklist to publish my speech. You can use it, too!

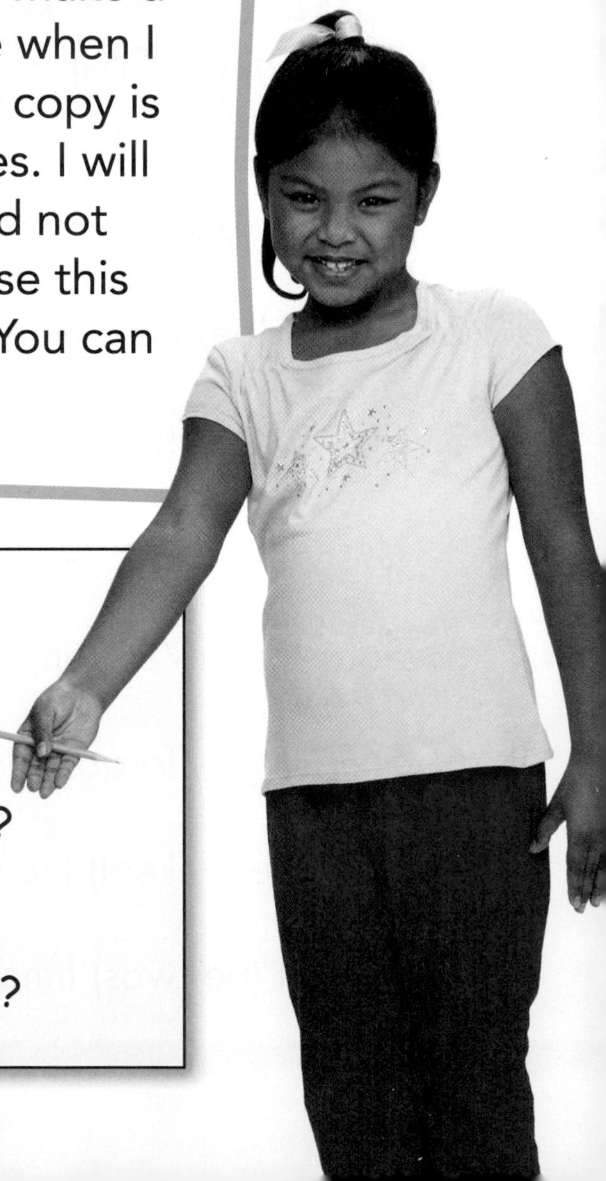

My Final Checklist

Did I—

✔ fix all my spelling mistakes?

✔ check the spelling of all the verbs?

✔ make a neat final copy?

✔ practice reading slowly and clearly?

FINAL DRAFT

Let's Fix Up Our Playground!

by Tashi

We should fix up our playground. One reason is that the swings are in bad shape. The squeaky chains are rusty. The seats are torn. The swings look terrible.

The second reason we should fix up our playground is that the slide is old and wobbly. It shakes when you climb it. Nobody wants to use it.

The third reason we should fix up our playground is that there are deep cracks in the basketball court. It is dangerous! Once someone fell down. Let's make our playground a safer place today!

Reflect

Did Tashi convince you to agree with her opinion? Which one of her reasons did you like best?

Opinion test writing

Read the Writing Prompt

Every writing test starts with a writing prompt. Most writing prompts have three parts:

Setup This tells what you need to know to get ready for writing.

Task This tells exactly what you're supposed to write.

Scoring Guide This part tells how your writing will be scored. You should include everything on the list to do well on the test.

A scoring guide is a lot like a rubric. It lists everything you need to think about to write a good paper. Many scoring guides will have the same parts as the rubrics we've looked at:

- Ideas
- Organization
- Voice
- Word Choice
- Sentence Fluency
- Conventions

Writing MODEL Prompt

An opinion is how you think or feel about something. You might think a dog is the best pet. Maybe you think baseball is the best sport. Do you have a favorite food?

What opinion would you like to share? Write an opinion paper about it. Give reasons and details.

Be sure your paper

- has a clear opinion and reasons.
- has a paragraph for each idea.
- uses a writer's voice that speaks to readers.
- uses well-chosen adjectives.
- has helpful transitions.
- has correct capitalization, punctuation, and spelling.

Writing Traits in the Scoring Guide

The scoring guide on page 287 has been made into this chart. How is it like the rubrics you've been using? Not all test prompts have the six writing traits. This one does!

Ideas	• **Be sure your paper has a clear opinion and reasons.**
Organization	• **Be sure your paper has a paragraph for each idea.**
Voice	• **Be sure your writer's voice speaks to the readers.**
Word Choice	• **Be sure your paper uses well-chosen adjectives.**
Sentence Fluency	• **Be sure your paper has helpful transitions.**
Conventions	• **Be sure your story has correct capitalization, punctuation, and spelling.**

Look at Justin Kern's paper. Did he follow the scoring guide?

Writing Prompt **MODEL** Response

The Best Snack

by Justin Kern

Apples are the best snacks. One reason is that they are easy to carry and eat. You can put one in a lunch bag or carry it in your backpack. When you're hungry, just take it out and munch.

You can never get bored with apples. There are so many different kinds. Some apples are sweet and juicy. Others can be tart and crisp.

Also, apples are good for you. They have vitamins you need to stay healthy. Have you heard? An apple a day keeps the doctor away!

Using the Scoring Guide to Study the Model

Now let's use the scoring guide to check Justin's writing test, "The Best Snack."

Ideas

- The paper has a clear opinion.

Justin's paper clearly states his opinion. I could tell from the very first sentence what he thinks are the best snacks.

Apples are the best snacks.

Organization

- The paper has a paragraph for each idea.

There are three paragraphs in Justin's paper. Each paragraph tells about one reason that Justin thinks apples are good snacks. Here's what the first paragraph tells about.

Apples are the best snack. One reason is that they are easy to carry and eat. You can put one in a lunch bag or carry it in your backpack. When you're hungry, just take it out and munch.

Voice

- The writer's voice speaks to the readers.

Justin uses the word *you* to speak directly to the readers. This makes his writing friendly. Justin could be talking right to me—or to you!

You can never get bored with apples.

Using the Scoring Guide to Study the Model

Word Choice

- The paper uses well-chosen adjectives.

Adjectives make writing more alive. They help readers see what you are talking about.

Justin used adjectives. He used the words *sweet, juicy, tart*, and *crisp*. I can almost taste the apples!

Some apples are sweet and juicy. Others can be tart and crisp.

Sentence Fluency

- The paper has transitions that help the readers.

Transition words are words such as *also, since*, and *because*. They show what one idea has to do with another. Justin used *Also*. It shows that he has more to say. Transition words also make sentences smoother.

Also, apples are good for you.

Conventions

- The capitalization, punctuation, and spelling are correct.

Justin did not make any mistakes at all in capitalization or punctuation. His final draft doesn't have any errors. Be sure to check your writing for any mistakes that you make often.

Many tests are timed. Your teacher will tell you how much time you have to take a test. Read the next two pages for some tips on how to plan your time and take a test.

Planning My Time

Look at the picture of the clock. Do you see that there is more green than any other color? That means you should spend most of your time getting ready to write. What takes the least amount of time?

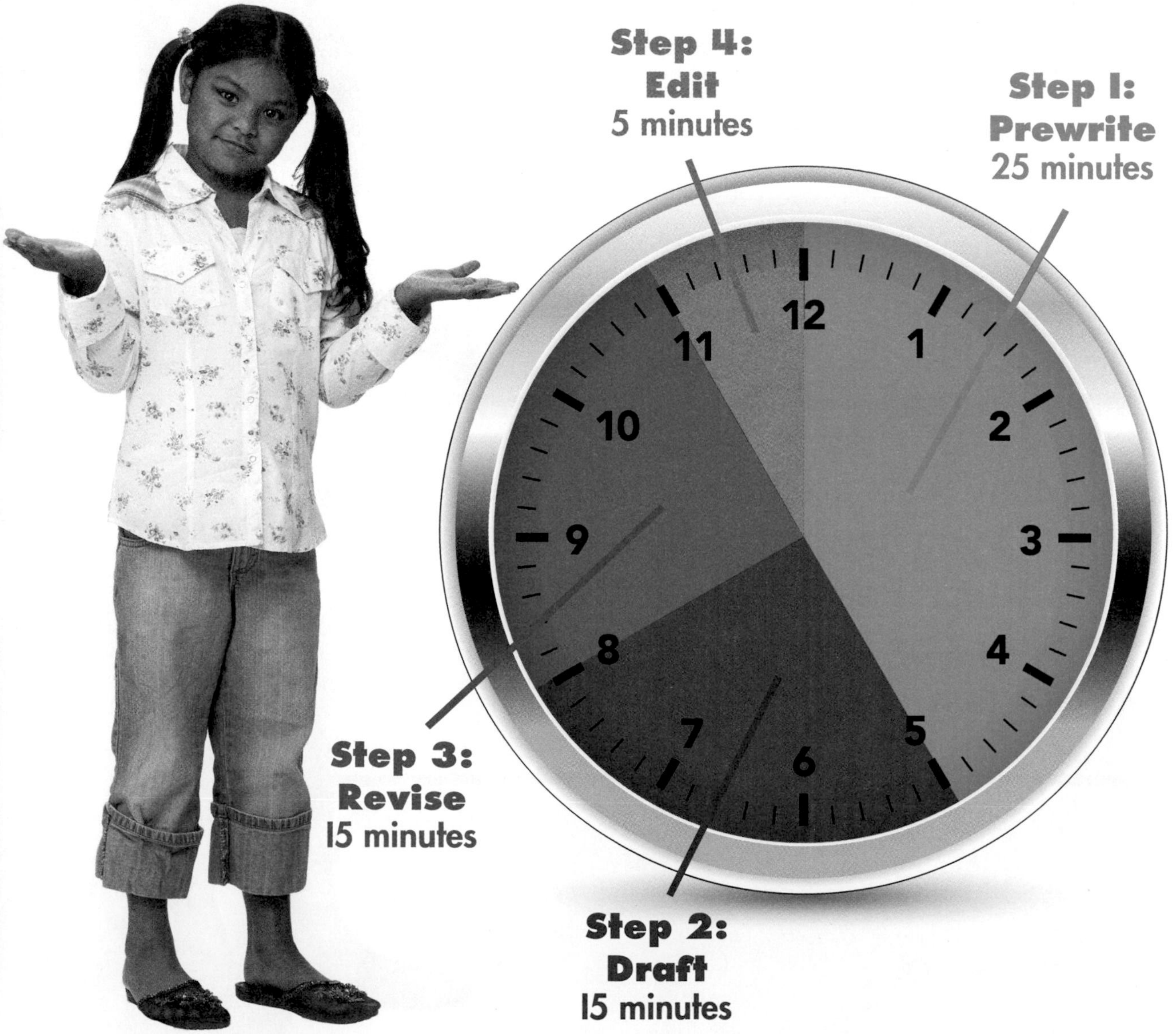

Remember these important tips when you write for a test.

Test Tips

1. **Study the writing prompt before you start to write.**
2. **Make sure you understand the task before you start to write.**
3. **Keep an eye on the clock.**
4. **Reread your writing. Compare it to the scoring guide at least twice.**
5. **Plan, plan, plan!**
6. **Write neatly.**

Writing an Opinion Test

Prewrite

Focus on Ideas

Writing Strategy Study the writing prompt and choose a topic.

First, I need to study the writing prompt. Then I will know what to do. See how I circled the important words in the task? These words tell me what I will write. The prompt says to write an opinion paper. I should give reasons and details to explain my opinion.

Then, I need to figure out what to write about. I have to think of an opinion I want to share. I think we need more recess time in school. I'll write an opinion paper about that. My paper will explain why I think this way.

My Writing Test Prompt

Setup — What opinion would you like to share? What would you like to change or keep the same?

Task — Write an opinion paper. Give reasons why you think as you do. Be sure to add details that support your reasons.

Here are my notes about an opinion I have. I think we should have longer recess at school. My paper will give reasons and details to support my opinion.

Notes

- We need longer recess
- Good exercise
- Healthy
- Play with others
- Make new friends
- Learn games
- Hopscotch and jump rope

Apply

Think about an opinion you have. Then write down some notes to help you get started.

Prewrite

Focus on **Organization**

Writing Strategy Make a graphic organizer.

I have some notes. Now I need to organize them. I can use a Network Tree. The topic goes at the top. In this paper, the topic is my opinion. The reasons go in the boxes under the topic. Details go in the boxes under the reasons.

Graphic Organizer: Network Tree

Topic: We Need Longer Recess

Reason 1
good exercise

Detail
keeps you healthy

Reason 2
play with others

Detail
make new friends

Reason 3
learn games

Detail
hopscotch and jump rope

Reflect

Look at Tashi's Network Tree. Does it organize her ideas? Will it help her write a good opinion paper?

Apply

Choose the best graphic organizer for the task. Organize your information.

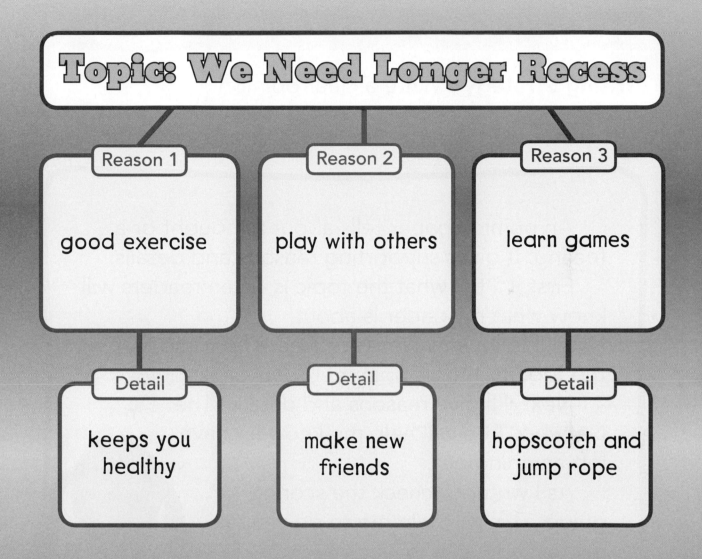

Draft

Focus on **Ideas**

Writing Strategy Write a clear opinion.

An opinion paper tells about a thought or a feeling. It gives supporting reasons and details.

First, I'll tell what the topic is. Then readers will know what my paper is about.

I'll follow my Network Tree. The topic is at the top. It tells my opinion.

Next, I'll give reasons and details. The Network Tree will help me know if I have left anything out.

As I write, I'll check the scoring guide. This will help me to do well on my test.

Proofreading Marks

/ Make a small letter
∧ Add something
ℓ Take out something
⊙ Add a period
≡ Make a capital letter

[DRAFT]

Kids Need Longer Recess!

by Tashi

my opinion

We need longer reces. One reason is to get exercise. This keeps people healthy. To much sitting at a desk is not good. you can also make friends.

Another reason is that recess lets us play together. In class we can't talk much to each other. It's great to have fun with other kids.

Recess is a good time to learn all kinds of games. I learned to play hopscotch and jump rope. Class time is important. Recess is good, too!

Reflect

Read the draft. Is Tashi's opinion clear?

Apply

Make sure your opinion is stated clearly.

Revise

Focus on **Ideas**

Writing Strategy Give reasons that support your opinion.

My opinion is what I think about my topic. Reasons explain my opinion. Details tell about the reasons.

I'll read my draft again. How I can make it better? I think I need another detail. I will add a detail about why exercise is important.

[DRAFT]

added a detail

We need longer reces. One reason is to get exercise. This keeps people healthy. Exercise builds strong muscles and bones. To much sitting at a desk is not good. you can also make friends.

Another reason is that recess lets us play together. In class we can't talk much to each other. It's great to have fun with other kids.

Recess is a good time to learn all kinds of games. I learned to play hopscotch and jump rope. Class time is important. Recess is good, too!

Reflect

Look at Tashi's revision. She added a detail about how exercise keeps people healthy. Does this make her paper clearer?

Apply

Make sure you give reasons and details that explain your opinion.

Revise

Focus on Organization

Writing Strategy Make sure each idea is in its own paragraph.

I'll read my paper again. This time I'll check the paragraphs. I'll make sure that each idea is in its own paragraph. A paragraph should tell about just one idea.

My first paragraph has two ideas. Most of it tells about exercise. But the last sentence is about friends. I can fix it. I can make the change right on my draft.

[DRAFT]

moved an idea

We need longer reces. One reason is to get exercise. This keeps people healthy. Exercise builds strong muscles and bones. To much sitting at a desk is not good. ~~you can also make friends.~~

Another reason is that recess lets us play together. In class we can't talk much to each other. It's great to have fun with other kids. you can also make friends.

Recess is a good time to learn all kinds of games. I learned to play hopscotch and jump rope. Class time is important. Recess is good, too!

Reflect

Look at Tashi's revision. Why did she move the sentence?

Apply

Check your draft. Make sure each paragraph is about just one idea.

Edit

Focus on Conventions

Writing Strategy Check the capitalization, punctuation, and spelling.

Sometimes I make spelling mistakes. My teacher told me to touch each word with my pencil. That helps me look at each word carefully.

I found two spelling mistakes and one capitalization mistake. I misspelled *recess* one time. Also, I wrote *to*. I meant to write *too*. I fixed all my mistakes.

Edits should be marked neatly. There is no time to make a final copy.

FINAL DRAFT

Kids Need Longer Recess!

by Tashi

We need longer recess. One reason is to get exercise. This keeps us ~~people~~ healthy. Exercise builds strong muscles and bones. Too much sitting at a desk is not good. ~~you can also make friends.~~

Another reason is that recess lets us play together. In class we can't talk much to each other. It's great to have fun with other kids. you can also make new friends.

Also, ~~R~~ecess is a good time to learn all kinds of fun games. I learned to play hopscotch and jump rope. Class time is important, but ~~R~~ecess is good, too!

Reflect

What do you think of Tashi's paper?

Apply

Check your capitalization, punctuation, and spelling.

Descriptive writing

makes a picture with words.

Hi! My name is Alisha. I live in Florida. I'm going to learn about descriptive writing. I'll use my five senses. I'll tell about what I see, hear, touch, taste, and smell. Keep reading to see how I will do it.

In this unit

- Descriptive Paper
- Descriptive Sketch
- MATH CONNECTION ▶ Poem
- Writing for a Test

Name: Alisha
Home: Florida
Hobbies: dancing, playing board games, skateboarding
Favorite Subject: language arts
Favorite Book: *Stuart Little* by E. B. White
Favorite Color: green

Parts of a Descriptive Paper

A descriptive paper tells about a person, place or thing. It can tell what I see, hear, touch, taste, or smell.

Introduction
The introduction is the beginning of my paper. I will tell what I am writing about.

Five Senses
I will use my five senses to describe what I see, hear, touch, taste, and smell.

Descriptive Words
Descriptive words paint a picture in the reader's mind. These words make my writing more interesting and help the reader imagine what something is like.

Body
The body is the middle of my paper. This is where I will describe a person, a place, or a thing.

Conclusion
This is the end of my paper. I can tell how I feel about my topic here, or I can end with an interesting detail.

Reasons for Writing a Descriptive Paper

Here are some reasons to write a descriptive paper.

To tell information
My grandma would love to hear about my new puppy. What does he look like? Does he have soft fur? I can tell all about him in a descriptive paper.

To remember
I can write about important things in a descriptive paper. If I describe my topic well, I can remember it clearly every time I read my paper.

To notice details
When I write a descriptive paper, I notice a lot more details than I usually do.

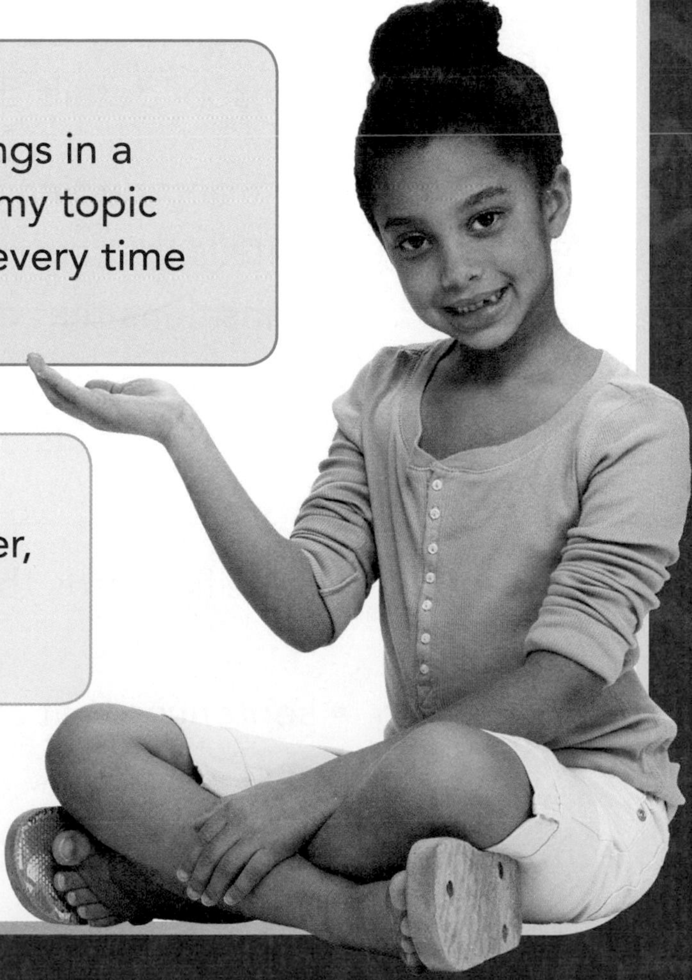

Linking Descriptive Writing Traits to a Descriptive Paper

In this chapter, you will describe a topic. This type of writing is called a descriptive paper. Alisha will guide you through the stages of the writing process. She will also show you some writing strategies that are linked to the Descriptive Writing Traits below.

Descriptive Writing Traits

Ideas	• a clear, focused topic • sensory details that tell readers about the topic
Organization	• a strong beginning, middle, and end • details that are in an order that makes sense • transitions that connect ideas
Voice	• a voice that fits the purpose and audience
Word Choice	• specific words that make a picture for the reader
Sentence Fluency	• sentences that are easy to read aloud
Conventions	• no or few errors in spelling, punctuation, and capitalization

Let's read this model of a descriptive paper. Andy tells about his puppy, Wrinkles. We will use the rubric to check his writing.

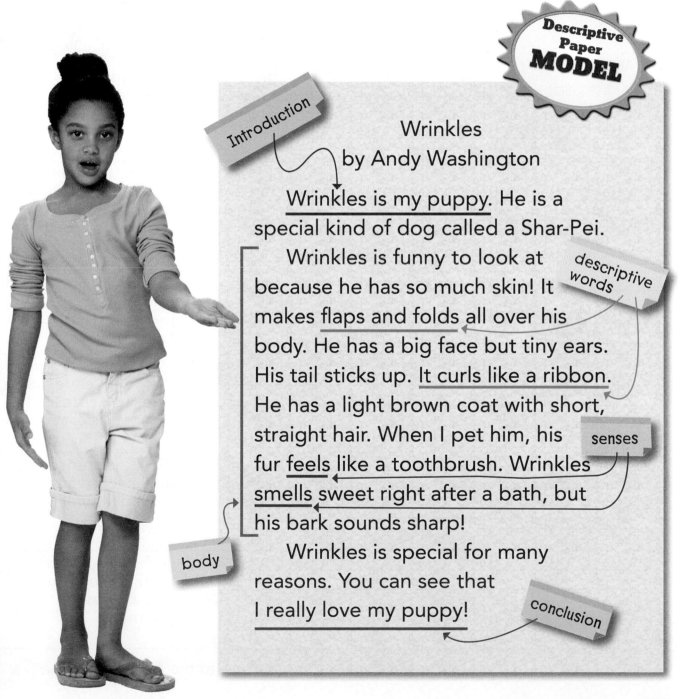

Descriptive Paper MODEL

Introduction

Wrinkles

by Andy Washington

Wrinkles is my puppy. He is a special kind of dog called a Shar-Pei.

Wrinkles is funny to look at because he has so much skin! It makes flaps and folds all over his body. He has a big face but tiny ears. His tail sticks up. It curls like a ribbon. He has a light brown coat with short, straight hair. When I pet him, his fur feels like a toothbrush. Wrinkles smells sweet right after a bath, but his bark sounds sharp!

descriptive words

senses

body

Wrinkles is special for many reasons. You can see that I really love my puppy!

conclusion

Descriptive Paper Rubric

	6	5	4
Ideas	The topic is clear and interesting with memorable details about all five senses.	The topic is interesting. The writer uses all five senses.	The topic is interesting. The writer uses two or three of the five senses.
Organization	The writer uses the five senses to organize the details. The writing is organized well.	Most of the details follow the five senses. The writing makes sense.	The writing generally makes sense. Details are not always organized with the senses.
Voice	The writer uses a personal "you" voice. The voice clearly belongs to this writer.	The writer generally uses a personal "you" voice and speaks to the reader.	The writer speaks to the reader some of the time.
Word Choice	Describing words and sensory information paint a clear picture.	Describing words help the reader use the five senses to picture the topic.	Most of the words help the reader use the five senses. The image is clear most of the time.
Sentence Fluency	The writing is smooth and natural. The sentences are easy to read and understand.	Most sentences are smooth and sound natural.	Some sentences are smooth and sound natural.
Conventions	The writer uses nouns and verbs correctly.	The writing contains minimal errors with nouns and verbs.	A few errors with nouns and verbs can be easily corrected.

+Presentation The title and the writer's name are at the top of the paper.

What makes a good descriptive paper? A rubric can help you decide. Use it to help you write. Then use it again to check your writing.

	3	2	1
Ideas	The topic could be more interesting. The writer uses one or two of the five senses.	The topic is confusing. Sensory details are sketchy.	The topic is not clear. Sensory information is missing.
Organization	Many of the details are out of order or unrelated to the topic.	The organization is confusing and does not help the reader understand the topic.	The writing is not organized and is a collection of random thoughts.
Voice	The writer's voice speaks to the reader and then fades.	The writer does not speak directly to the reader. The writer's voice is faint.	The writing lacks voice.
Word Choice	Some of the words help the reader use the fives senses.	Words are vague or do not use the five senses to describe.	The word choice feels random and does not describe.
Sentence Fluency	Some of the writing is difficult to understand.	A few sentences are confusing. The meaning is not clear.	Many sentences are choppy or too long. The piece is difficult to read.
Conventions	Errors with nouns and verbs confuse the reader.	Many errors with nouns and verbs stop the reader from understanding.	Serious, frequent errors make the writing very hard to understand.

See Appendix B for 4-, 5-, and 6-point descriptive rubrics.

Using the Descriptive Paper Rubric to Study the Model

Let's use the rubric to check Andy's descriptive paper about Wrinkles.

Ideas

- The topic is clear and interesting with memorable details about all five senses.

Andy makes his topic interesting. He uses many memorable details about his puppy. Here he tells how Wrinkles smells and sounds.

> Wrinkles smells sweet right after a bath, but his bark sounds sharp!

Organization

- The writer uses the five senses to organize the details.
- The writing is organized well.

Andy first writes about how Wrinkles looks. Then he tells how Wrinkles feels, smells, and sounds. Here's what Andy wrote about the sense of touch.

When I pet him, his fur feels like a toothbrush.

Voice

- The writer uses a personal "you" voice.
- The voice clearly belongs to this writer.

Andy gives the reader great examples of why Wrinkles is special. When he uses *you*, I feel like he is talking right to me!

Wrinkles is special for many reasons. You can see that I really love my puppy!

Word Choice

- Describing words and sensory information paint a clear picture.

There are many descriptive words in the paper. Here's an example that helps us picture the puppy's tail.

> His tail sticks up. It curls like a ribbon.

Sentence Fluency

- The writing is smooth and natural.
- The sentences are easy to read and understand.

Andy's paper is fun to read and easy to follow. His sentences are smooth and natural. This sentence uses the transition word *because*. It connects ideas smoothly.

> Wrinkles is funny to look at because he has so much skin!

Conventions

- The writer uses nouns and verbs correctly.

Andy uses nouns and verbs to give a clear picture of his puppy. Here he uses the nouns *flaps* and *folds*. They describe Wrinkles' skin. Can you see how Wrinkles got his name?

It makes flaps and folds all over his body.

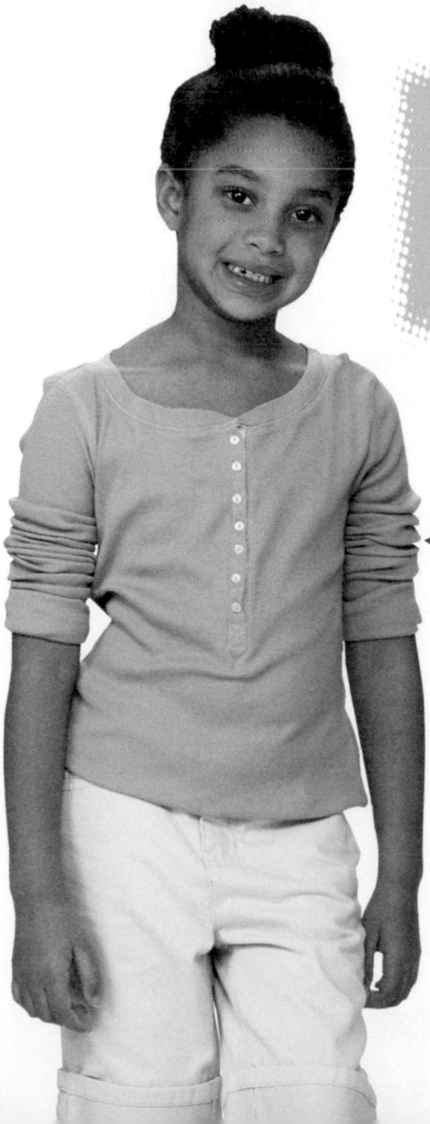

+Presentation The title and the writer's name are at the top of the paper.

My Turn!

Now it's my turn. I'm going to write my own descriptive paper. Read on to see how I will do it.

Prewrite

Focus on **Ideas**

The Rubric Says The topic is clear and interesting with memorable details about all five senses.

Writing Strategy Choose a topic. Make a list of interesting details about it.

Before I start writing, I need to pick a topic that will be interesting to my readers. There's an unusual food market in my neighborhood. It would be a great topic for my paper! I'll make a list of information about the Super T. Then I'll write some details about each thing on my list.

Writer's Term

Topic

The **topic** of a paper is what you will write about.

My List	What I Know
interesting fruits, like mangoes and kiwis	how they look, feel, and smell
strings of chili peppers	how they look and smell
herbs and spices	how they look and smell
people talking in a lot of different languages	how they look and sound
music playing	how it sounds
cash register beeping	how it sounds

Reflect

Look at Alisha's details. Does she include enough information to write a paper?

Apply

Choose a topic. Then write details that describe the topic.

Prewrite

Focus on **Organization**

The Rubric Says The writer uses the five senses to organize the details.

Writing Strategy Make a Five-Senses Chart to organize your notes.

Next I need to organize my notes. The rubric says my paper should be organized using the five senses. A Five-Senses Chart can help me do that. I will write all the things I can see on one part of my chart. I will do the same with what I can hear, taste, touch, and smell.

Writer's Term

Five-Senses Chart

A **Five-Senses Chart** helps you organize things based on how they look, sound, taste, feel, and smell.

Graphic Organizer: Five-Senses Chart

Topic: The Super T	
I can **see**	• mangoes and kiwis • strings of chili peppers • herbs and spices • many people
I can **hear**	• people talking • music playing • cash register beeping
I can **taste**	• I can't taste anything at the Super T unless I buy it.
I can **touch** (feel)	• mangoes and kiwis
I can **smell**	• mangoes and kiwis • strings of chili peppers • herbs and spices

Reflect

How will the Five-Senses Chart help Alisha write a good paper?

Apply

Make a Five-Senses Chart for your own topic. List enough details to use in your paper.

Draft

Focus on **Ideas**

The Rubric Says The topic is clear and interesting with memorable details about all five senses.

Writing Strategy Use sentences with sensory details.

Next I'll begin a draft of my descriptive paper. The rubric says I should include a lot of details. I'll use my Five-Senses Chart. It will help me decide what to write about the market. I won't worry if I make mistakes. I can fix them when I edit.

Proofreading Marks

- / Make a small letter
- ∧ Add something
- Take out something
- ⊙ Add a period
- ≡ Make a capital letter

[DRAFT]

The Super T is a food market on my street it is filled with great food!

I can see strings of chili peppers. Fruits and vegetables in the front. I can smell the mangoes and the peppers. I can also smell fresh herbs and spices for cooking. I can feel the mangoes and the kiwis.

In the Super T, I can hear people talking in different languages. The Super T is a great place!

Senses

Senses

Reflect

Read Alisha's draft. Which senses has she used? Which sense did she leave out?

Apply

Use your Five-Senses Chart to write your draft.

Revise

Focus on **Ideas**

The Rubric Says The topic is clear and interesting with memorable details about all five senses.

Writing Strategy Use interesting details.

After I write my draft, I'll read it again. Then I'll revise it. That means I will change my draft to make my writing better. The rubric says that I need to use memorable details. I will try to add words that help readers picture and remember the market.

[DRAFT]

The Super T is a food market on my street it is filled with great food!

I can see strings of chili peppers. Fruits and vegetables in the front. I can smell the mangoes and the peppers. I can also smell fresh herbs and spices for cooking. I can feel the mangoes and the kiwis.

In the Super T, I can hear people talking in different languages. There's more. Music plays. The cash register beeps. The Super T is a great place!

added interesting details

Reflect

Look at the details Alisha added. How do they help you picture the market?

Apply

Now look at your draft. Where can you add details to help your readers picture your topic?

Revise

Focus on **Organization**

The Rubric Says The writing is organized well.

Writing Strategy Make sure the details are organized in a way that makes sense.

I will read my paper again to make sure I did all of the things in the rubric. It says that my writing should be well organized. That means that the details should all be in the order that makes sense. I see that I need to move a sentence so that my writing makes sense. Do you agree?

[DRAFT]

The Super T is a food market on my street it is filled with great food!

Fruits and vegetables in the front.

I can see strings of chili peppers.

~~Fruits and vegetables in the front.~~

I can smell the mangoes and the peppers.

moved to organize details

Reflect

Look at the sentence Alisha moved. How does it help organize her paper better?

Apply

Look at your draft. Are your details in the best order? Do you need to move any sentences?

Edit

Focus on Conventions

The Rubric Says The writer uses nouns and verbs correctly.

Writing Strategy Use nouns and verbs correctly.

Now it's time to edit my paper. I need to check my spelling. I also need to make sure each sentence starts with a capital letter and ends with punctuation. Also I must check to see that I used nouns and verbs correctly. Every sentence must have a noun and a verb.

Writer's Term

Nouns and Verbs

Nouns are words for people, places, or things. Some **verbs** tell actions, such as **look** or **spin**.

[DRAFT]

The Super T is a food market on my street. it is filled with great food! Fruits and vegetables are in the front. ~~I~~ You can see strings of red, green, and purple chili peppers. ~~Fruits and vegetables in the front.~~ ~~I~~ you can smell the sweet mangoes and the spicy peppers.

added a verb

Reflect

Does every sentence have at least one noun and one verb?

Apply

Now edit your own draft. Correct punctuation and capitalization. Be sure that you have used nouns and verbs correctly. For practice with nouns and verbs, see the next two pages.

Nouns

Know the Rule

A **noun** is the name of a person, place, or thing.
Example: What is in that **box**?

Practice the Rule

Write the numbers 1–8 on a separate sheet of paper. Read the sentences below. Write the noun you find in each sentence.

1. You can open the present.
2. It is inside that large box.
3. I want it to be a surprise.
4. I will not give you any clues.
5. You can tell that it is not a bicycle.
6. Yesterday we bought it in the city.
7. We rode there on the train.
8. We enjoyed choosing your gift.

Verbs

Know the Rule

Verbs are words that tell the action in a sentence. Every sentence must have a verb.

Example: Jack and Sasha **swim** almost every day in the summer.

Practice the Rule

Write the numbers 1–8 on a separate sheet of paper. Read the sentences below. Write the verb you find in each sentence.

1. Our kittens play with each other.
2. One kitten hides under the bed.
3. The other kitten chases the toy mouse.
4. Sometimes I hold both kittens on my lap.
5. One kitten purrs a lot.
6. I call her Rumbles.
7. The other kitten runs very fast.
8. He also jumps a lot.

Publish

+Presentation

Publishing Strategy Post the paper on the classroom bulletin board.

Presentation Strategy Put the title and your name on the paper.

My descriptive paper is done! Now, it's time to publish it. I'll make a neat final copy. When I do, I'll write the title and my name at the top. Then, I'll share it by posting it on our classroom bulletin board. I will use this checklist to publish my paper. You can use it to check your final draft, too.

My Final Checklist

Did I —

- ✔ use correct punctuation and capitalization?
- ✔ check my spelling?
- ✔ use nouns and verbs correctly?
- ✔ put my title and name on my paper?

FINAL DRAFT

The Super T

by Alisha

The Super T is a food market on my street. It is filled with great food! It is a large store with bright lights.

Fruits and vegetables are in the front. You can see strings of red, green, and purple chili peppers. You can smell the sweet mangoes and the spicy peppers. You can also smell fresh herbs and spices for cooking. You can feel the smooth mangoes and the fuzzy kiwis.

In the Super T, you can hear people talking in different languages. There's music playing, and the cash register beeps.

The Super T is a great place!

Reflect

Look at Alisha's paper. Then use the rubric to check your own paper.

Parts of a Descriptive Sketch

A descriptive sketch is a paper I write about a person, a place, or a thing in my life.

Narrator
A narrator is the person who tells about the topic. In a descriptive sketch, I'm the narrator!

Introduction
The introduction is at the beginning of my sketch. It tells what I'm going to write about.

Body
This is the main part of my sketch. I will give lots of details about my topic in this part.

Conclusion
This is the end of the paper. I will sum up what I want the reader to know about my topic.

Reasons for Writing a Descriptive Sketch

Here are some reasons to write a descriptive sketch.

To tell information
A descriptive sketch is a great way to tell about someone or something that is special to you. You can tell the reader all kinds of information!

To remember
Someday I might want to remember something or someone special. A descriptive sketch will help me remember that thing or person clearly.

To notice details
A descriptive sketch can be fun to read because it usually includes a lot of interesting details about the topic. It can be funny or surprising, too.

Linking Descriptive Writing Traits to a Descriptive Sketch

In this chapter, you will describe a person, place, or thing in your life. This type of writing is called a descriptive sketch. Alisha will guide you through the stages of the writing process. She will also show you some writing strategies that are linked to the Descriptive Writing Traits below.

Descriptive Writing Traits

Ideas	• a clear, focused topic • sensory details that tell readers about the topic
Organization	• a strong beginning, middle, and end • details that are in an order that makes sense • transitions that connect ideas
Voice	• a voice that fits the purpose and audience
Word Choice	• specific words that make a picture for the reader
Sentence Fluency	• sentences that are easy to read aloud
Conventions	• no or few errors in spelling, punctuation, and capitalization

Let's look at this model of a descriptive sketch. Gabe tells us about his best friend, Nick. We will use the rubric to check his writing.

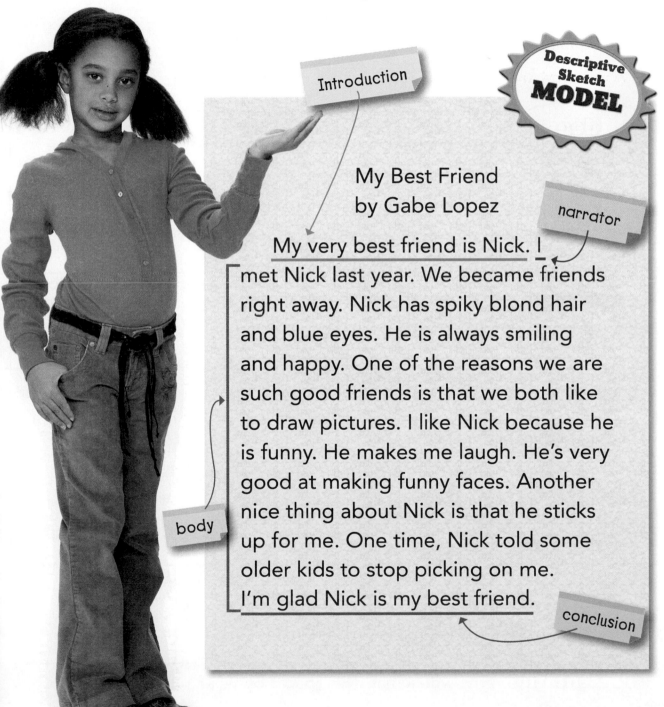

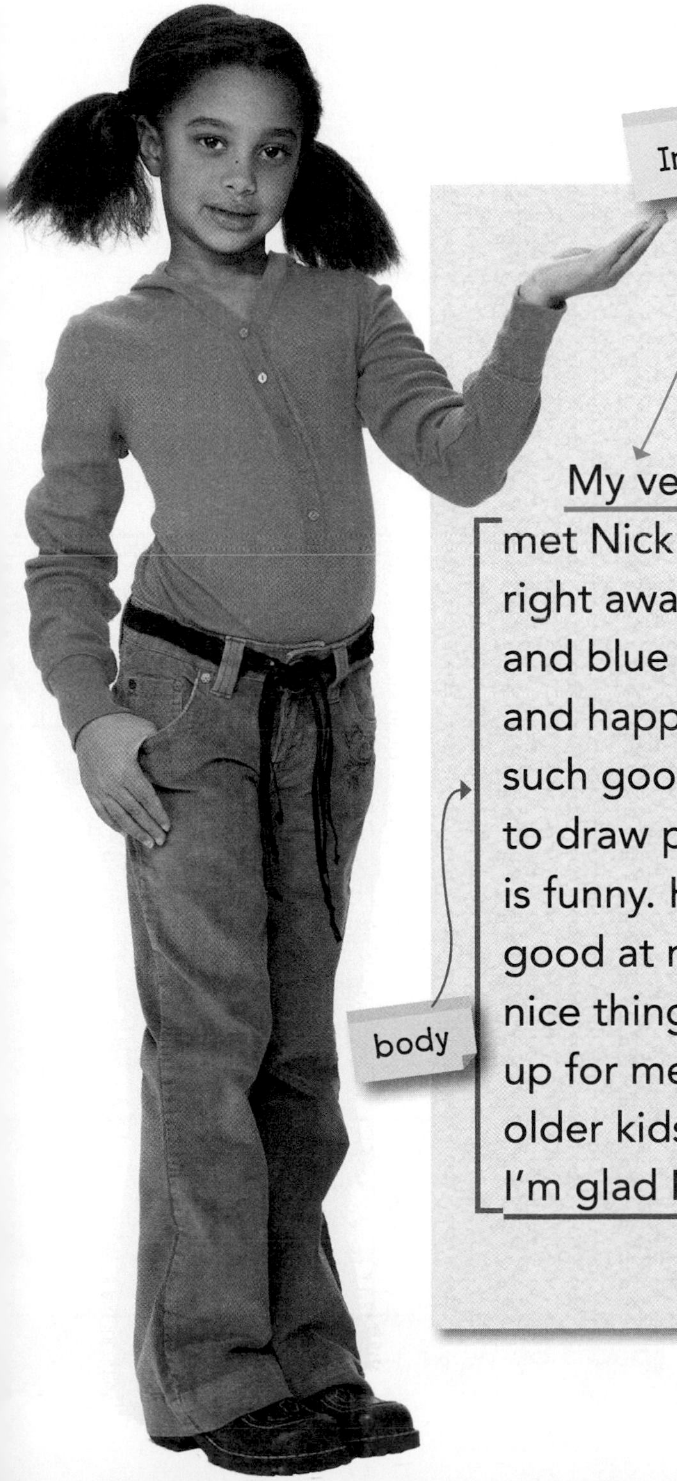

Descriptive Sketch MODEL

Introduction

narrator

body

conclusion

My Best Friend
by Gabe Lopez

My very best friend is Nick. I met Nick last year. We became friends right away. Nick has spiky blond hair and blue eyes. He is always smiling and happy. One of the reasons we are such good friends is that we both like to draw pictures. I like Nick because he is funny. He makes me laugh. He's very good at making funny faces. Another nice thing about Nick is that he sticks up for me. One time, Nick told some older kids to stop picking on me. I'm glad Nick is my best friend.

Descriptive Sketch Rubric

	6	5	4
Ideas	Carefully selected details make the subject memorable.	The subject is interesting. All details help the reader "see" the subject.	The subject is interesting. Most details help the reader "see" the subject.
Organization	The organization of the writing gives the reader a clear and memorable descriptive sketch.	The sketch includes a strong introduction, a detailed body, and a strong conclusion.	The sketch is organized. The introduction or the conclusion could be stronger.
Voice	The writer clearly knows the subject and helps the reader know it, too.	The writer likes the subject and wants the reader to know the subject, too.	The writer's voice sounds enthusiastic most of the time. The reader can easily know the subject.
Word Choice	Describing words are strong and clear. They help the reader "see" the topic.	Describing words bring the subject to life. The sketch is fun to read.	Most words help the reader "see" the subject. The reader can figure out the picture.
Sentence Fluency	The right number of contractions make the sentences smooth, natural, and easy to read.	One or two more contractions would make the sentences flow better.	A few errors with contractions interrupt the flow of the sentences.
Conventions	Apostrophes are used correctly to create understanding.	A few errors with apostrophes can be easily corrected.	Some errors with apostrophes confuse the reader.

+Presentation The writing has even spaces between words and lines.

What makes a good descriptive sketch? A rubric can help you decide. Use it to help you write. Then use it again to check your writing.

3	2	1	
The subject could be more interesting. Some details do not describe the subject.	The subject is not clear. The details may not belong together.	The writing lacks details to create a clear subject.	Ideas
The introduction or the conclusion are incomplete or missing.	The sketch is not organized into separate parts.	The writing lacks any organization. It is just a collection of random thoughts.	Organization
The writer's voice comes and goes. The reader must work hard to know the subject.	The writer's voice seems uninterested in the subject.	The voice is very weak and uninterested. The reader cannot learn about the subject.	Voice
A few words describe the subject. The reader cannot form a clear picture.	The words tell about a subject. The words do not describe the subject with accuracy.	The word choice feels random or accidental. The words do not describe.	Word Choice
Too many contractions confuse the reader and make the sentences choppy.	No contractions are used. Many sentences do not flow.	Some sentences are incomplete. Sentences do not flow.	Sentence Fluency
Many errors with apostrophes make the reader struggle to understand.	Numerous errors with apostrophes get in the way of understanding.	Serious, frequent errors with apostrophes make the writing hard to understand.	Conventions

See Appendix B for 4-, 5-, and 6-point descriptive rubrics.

Using the Descriptive Sketch Rubric to Study the Model

Let's use the rubric to check Gabe's descriptive sketch about his best friend, Nick.

Ideas

- Carefully selected details make the subject memorable.

Gabe uses details that help me get to know Nick. Here is a detail that I really like. It will help me remember what a good person Nick is.

> One time, Nick told some older kids to stop picking on me.

Organization

- The organization of the writing gives the reader a clear and memorable descriptive sketch.

Gabe included all of these parts: introduction, body, and conclusion. At the beginning, he tells what happened when he and Nick first met. Gabe gives a good, clear time order to the whole character sketch.

> I met Nick last year. We became friends right away.

Voice

- The writer clearly knows the subject and helps the reader know it, too.

I can tell by the way Gabe writes that he knows and likes Nick. Gabe has good reasons that he and Nick are such good friends.

> One of the reasons we are such good friends is that we both like to draw pictures.

Word Choice

- Describing words are strong and clear. They help the reader "see" the topic.

Gabe uses great describing words, such as *spiky*. They give me a clear picture of his friend Nick.

> Nick has spiky blond hair and blue eyes.

Sentence Fluency

- The right number of contractions makes the sentences smooth, natural, and easy to read.

Gabe uses contractions in a natural way in this descriptive sketch. I like the way he has used one in his conclusion.

> I'm glad Nick is my best friend.

Conventions

- Apostrophes are used correctly to create understanding.

Gabe uses apostrophes correctly in his sketch. I can understand this sentence very well.

He's very good at making funny faces.

Presentation The writing has even spaces between words and lines.

My Turn!

Now it's my turn. I'm going to write my own descriptive sketch. Read on to see how I will do it.

Prewrite

Focus on **Ideas**

The Rubric Says Carefully selected details make the subject memorable.

Writing Strategy Make notes to answer questions that readers may ask about the topic.

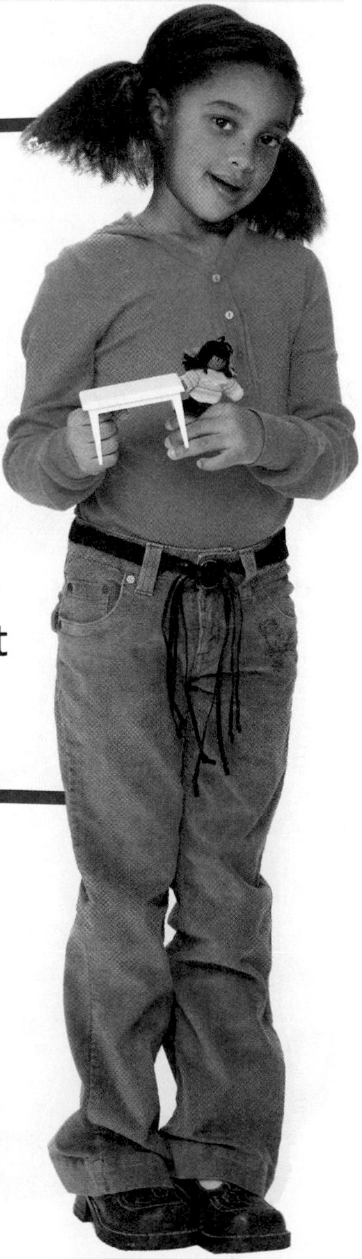

Before writing my descriptive sketch, I'll pick a topic. I want to write about my favorite toy. Everybody likes toys! First, I'll make a list of questions readers may have about my topic. Then, I'll write notes to answer the questions. My answers should have details that readers will want to remember. I'll try to tell what is special about my favorite toy.

Writer's Term

Topic

The **topic** is what or who the sketch is about.

My Favorite Toy

Questions	Answers
What is your favorite toy?	my dollhouse
When did you get the toy?	on my fifth birthday
What does the toy look like?	white with a green door
What does it have or do?	doorbell that rings windows that open lots of rooms tiny lamps, beds, tables, bathtub mom, dad, baby dolls
Why is the toy special?	because it belonged to my mom

Reflect

Look at Alisha's notes. Does she have enough information to write a good descriptive sketch?

Apply

Make a list of some questions about your topic. Then write the answers.

Prewrite

Focus on **Organization**

The Rubric Says The organization of the writing gives the reader a clear and memorable descriptive sketch.

Writing Strategy Make an Attribute Chart to organize the introduction, body, and conclusion.

All writing should have a beginning, a middle, and an end. Those parts are called the introduction, the body, and the conclusion. I'll make an Attribute Chart to organize the information from my question and answer notes. Then I'll write where each note belongs in the chart.

Writer's Term

Attribute Chart

An **Attribute Chart** gives details about many parts of a person or thing.

Graphic Organizer: Attribute Chart

My Favorite Toy	
Introduction What is my favorite toy?	• my dollhouse
Body When did I get the toy?	• on my fifth birthday
Body What does it look like?	• white with a green door
Body What does it have?	• doorbell that rings • windows that open • lots of rooms • tiny lamps, beds, tables, bathtub • mom, dad, baby dolls
Conclusion Why is it special?	• because it belonged to my mom

Reflect

Look at Alisha's Attribute Chart. How will it help her write a descriptive sketch?

Apply

Make an Attribute Chart for your topic. Think about the information you want in your introduction, body, and conclusion.

Draft

Focus on Organization

The Rubric Says	The organization of the writing gives the reader a clear and memorable descriptive sketch.
Writing Strategy	Use details to develop the introduction and body.

Next I'll use my question and answer notes and my Attribute Chart to write a draft. The rubric says to organize my sketch so it is clear and memorable. Good writing starts with an introduction. The introduction tells what the writing will be about. The body tells all the details about the topic. The last thing my readers will read is the conclusion. It needs to be something that they will remember.

Proofreading Marks

- / Make a small letter
- ∧ Add something
- ℓ Take out something
- ⊙ Add a period
- ≡ Make a capital letter

[DRAFT]

introduced the topic

information about topic

memorable details

My Favorite Toy

My favorite toy is my dollhouse. It was my mothers dollhouse when she was a girl. I got it on my fifth birthday. I can open and close the windows. There are tiny lamps and tables. It even has a little bathtub! Theres a kitchen. I have a mommy, daddy, and baby doll that live in the house. It is a fun toy to share with my friends. The dollhouse is special.

Reflect

Does Alisha tell the topic in the introduction? What details tell more about the topic?

Apply

Use your chart to write the first draft of your descriptive sketch. Begin by introducing your topic.

Revise

Focus on **Voice**

The Rubric Says The writer clearly knows the subject and helps the reader know it, too.

Writing Strategy Sound as if you know and care about the topic.

Now I'll read my draft to see if I can make it better. The rubric says that I should sound like I know my topic very well. I also want to let my readers know that I feel strongly about my topic. Look at the sentence I added. Can you tell how I feel about the dollhouse?

[DRAFT]

My favorite toy is my dollhouse. It was my mothers dollhouse when she was a girl. I got it on my fifth birthday. It has a doorbell that really rings! I can open and close the windows. There are tiny lamps and tables. It even has a little bathtub!

showed strong feeling

Reflect

What details did Alisha add to her descriptive sketch? How did this make her writing voice stronger?

Apply

Now look at your draft. What can you add to show that you know and care about your topic?

Revise

Focus on Word Choice

The Rubric Says Describing words are strong and clear. They help the reader "see" the topic.

Writing Strategy Add descriptive words or details.

The rubric reminds me to use clear, strong words to describe my dollhouse. I want to describe exactly what my dollhouse is like so my readers can imagine it. The more helpful details I add, the more my readers will enjoy my writing!

[DRAFT]

My favorite toy is my dollhouse. It was my mothers dollhouse when she was a girl. I got it on my fifth birthday. It is white with a green door. It has a doorbell that really rings! I can open and close the windows. There are tiny lamps and tables. It even has a little bathtub! Theres a kitchen. I have a mommy, daddy, and baby doll that live in the house. It's a fun toy to share with my friends. The dollhouse is special.

added descriptive details

Reflect

Look at the words Alisha added. How does she help you picture her dollhouse?

Apply

Look at your draft. Where can you add clear, strong describing words?

Edit

Focus on Conventions

The Rubric Says Apostrophes are used correctly to create understanding.

Writing Strategy Make sure that apostrophes are used correctly.

The next step is to edit my descriptive sketch. I'll make sure that my spelling and punctuation are correct. I will make sure I have apostrophes in contractions. Contractions make my writing sound like the way I talk. I will use them to show possession, too.

Writer's Term

Apostrophe

An **apostrophe** takes the place of missing letters in a contraction, as in **I'm**. An apostrophe also shows possession, as in **Sam's book**.

[DRAFT]

added apostrophe

My favorite toy is my dollhouse. It was my mother's dollhouse when she was a girl. I got it on my fifth birthday. It is white with a green door.

Reflect

Where did Alisha add an apostrophe? Why did she add it?

Apply

Make sure to check the places in your writing where you should use apostrophes. For more practice with apostrophes, turn to the next two pages.

Apostrophes

Know the Rule

A **contraction** is made up of two words that are put together. Some letters from the two words are left out. An **apostrophe** takes the place of the missing letters.

Examples:	did not	didn't
	will not	won't
	we will	we'll

Practice the Rule

Write the numbers 1–6 on a separate sheet of paper. Write the contraction for the two underlined words in each sentence.

1. Li does not want to write about her sister.
2. She will write about her dog.
3. I will read the draft of her descriptive sketch.
4. Gina is not sure about her topic either.
5. She could not decide between her bike and her skates.
6. I am going to write about my big brother.

More Apostrophes

Know the Rule

A noun that shows ownership is called a **possessive noun**. Use an **apostrophe** plus *s* to show ownership.

Examples: bird's, family's, puppy's, musician's, flower's, father's

Practice the Rule

Write the numbers 1–6 on a separate sheet of paper. Write the possessive form of the underlined word in each sentence.

1. The <u>writer</u> story made me laugh.
2. It was about an <u>animal</u> mixed-up adventure.
3. The <u>creature</u> body had parts from many different animals.
4. It had an <u>elephant</u> trunk and the ears of a donkey.
5. It had a <u>lion</u> mane and the eyes of a frog.
6. The <u>artist</u> drawings of the creature were very funny.

Publish

+Presentation

Publishing Strategy Add the sketch to a class album.

Presentation Strategy Check the spacing between words and lines.

I finished my descriptive sketch! Next I'll make a neat final copy for our class album. I'll be careful with spaces between words and lines. Neat spacing will make my writing easier to read. I'll use the checklist to make sure I'm ready to publish my sketch. You can use the checklist to check your final draft, too.

My Final Checklist

Did I —

✔ use capital letters correctly?

✔ use apostrophes correctly?

✔ check my spacing between words and lines?

✔ include the title and my name?

FINAL DRAFT

My Favorite Toy

by Alisha

My favorite toy is my dollhouse. It was my mother's dollhouse when she was a girl. I got it for my fifth birthday. It is white with a green door. It has a doorbell that really rings! I can open and close the windows. There are tiny lamps and tables. It even has a little bathtub! The kitchen has a shiny stove with four burners. I have a mommy, daddy, and baby doll that live in the house. It's a fun toy to share with my friends. The dollhouse is special in my family. I will give it to my children someday.

Reflect

Use the rubric to check your final draft.

Parts of a Poem

A poem is a special kind of writing. Some poems have special shapes. Other poems rhyme or have a beat.

Lines
A poem does not have paragraphs. It may not have sentences. A poem has lines. Lines may be long or short.

Stanzas
Some poems have more than one group of lines. These groups are called *stanzas*.

Rhyme
Some poems have rhyming words. Rhyming words, such as *go* and *know*, end with the same sound.

Repetition
Some poems have words or lines that are used more than once. Repeating words and lines give the poem a special feeling.

Reasons for Writing a Poem

Here are some reasons to write a poem.

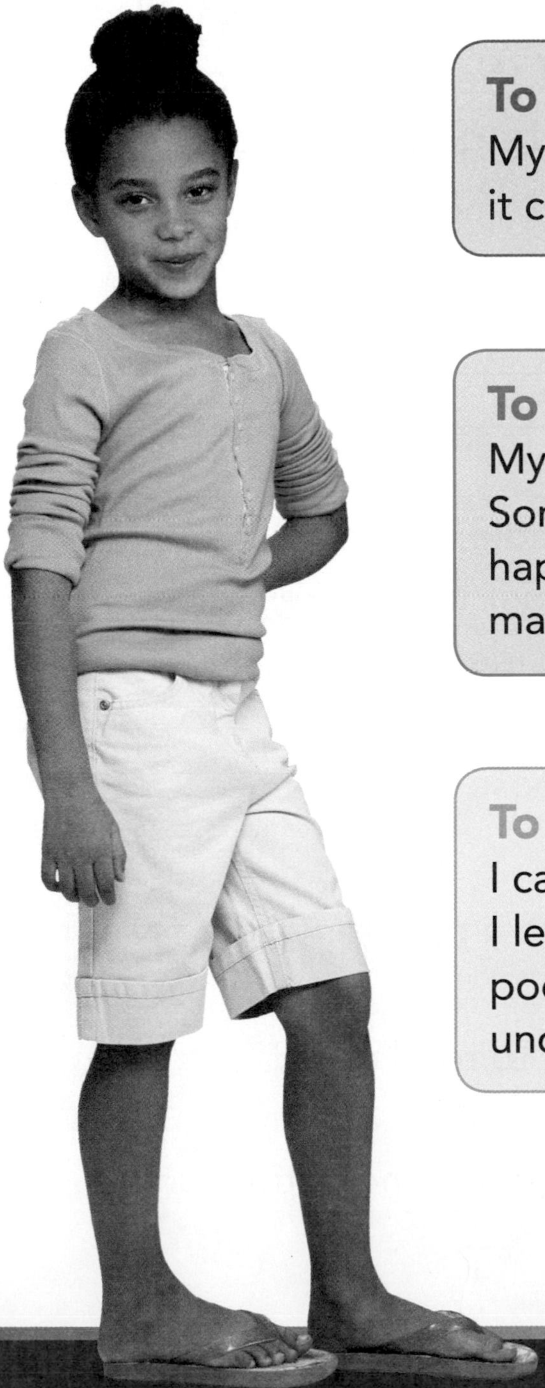

To describe
My poem could describe a tree. Or it could describe a person or a party.

To share feelings
My poem can tell how I feel. Some poems make people feel happy or sad. Some poems make people want to laugh.

To understand
I can tell what I have learned. When I learn something new, I can write a poem. My poem might help others understand, too.

Linking Descriptive Writing Traits to a Poem

In this chapter, you will write a poem. Alisha will guide you through the stages of the writing process. She will also show you some writing strategies that are linked to the Descriptive Writing Traits below.

Descriptive Writing Traits

Ideas	• a clear, focused topic • sensory details that tell readers about the topic
Organization	• a strong beginning, middle, and end • details that are in an order that makes sense • transitions that connect ideas
Voice	• a voice that fits the purpose and audience
Word Choice	• specific words that make a picture for the reader
Sentence Fluency	• sentences that are easy to read aloud
Conventions	• no or few errors in spelling, punctuation, and capitalization

Let's read this model of a poem. Conrad helps his readers understand which container holds more. We can use the rubric to check his writing.

Poem MODEL

Which Holds More?
by Conrad Morris

Open the cupboard door; what do you see?
I see boxes … staring at me.
Big box, little box, which holds more?
That big yellow box, just inside the door
Holds more…
NOODLES!

Open the fridge door; what do you see?
I see bottles … staring at me.
Tall bottle, short bottle, which holds more?
That tall, cold bottle, just inside the door
Holds more…
JUICE!

repetition

rhyming words

two stanzas

lines

Poem Rubric

	6	5	4
Ideas	The writer uses specific details to make a clear picture for the reader.	The writer uses details that create a clear picture for the reader.	Most of the details create a clear picture.
Organization	The poem's form or shape makes the ideas clear for the reader.	The poem's form or shape fits the subject.	The poem's form or shape could fit the subject better.
Voice	The voice is original and enthusiastic.	The voice is original and enthusiastic most of the time.	The voice is original and enthusiastic some of the time.
Word Choice	The words chosen for the poem are strong and clear.	Descriptive words help the reader "see" the subject.	Most words help the reader "see" the subject.
Sentence Fluency	The poem sounds natural and smooth. It is easy to read.	Each word or line flows into the next. The poem is fairly easy to read.	Most of the lines are smooth. A few lines are hard to read.
Conventions	Sentences use adjectives and adverbs correctly to create meaning.	A few errors with complete adjectives and adverbs can be easily corrected.	Some errors with adjectives and adverbs confuse the reader.

+Presentation The poem is neat and legible.

What makes a good poem? A rubric can help you decide. Use it to help you write. Then use it again to check your writing.

	3	2	1
Ideas	Few details create a clear picture.	Details may not belong together. They confuse the reader.	There are no useful details and the reader is confused.
Organization	The poem's form or shape does not fit the subject.	The writing is not in poem form.	The writing is a collection of random thoughts and is not a poem.
Voice	The voice sounds distant or uninterested.	The voice is not clear or is absent.	The piece lacks any voice from the writer.
Word Choice	Few words help the reader "see" the subject.	The words do not describe. Some may be used incorrectly.	The word choice is random or incorrect.
Sentence Fluency	Some of the words or lines are choppy.	Most of the writing is choppy. The poem is hard to read.	The writing is not in poem form.
Conventions	Many errors with adjectives and adverbs make the reader struggle to understand.	Numerous errors with adjectives and adverbs get in the way of understanding.	Serious, frequent errors with adjectives and adverbs make the writing hard to understand.

See Appendix B for 4-, 5-, and 6-point descriptive rubrics.

Using the Poem Rubric to Study the Model

Let's use the rubric to check Conrad's poem about which container holds more.

Ideas

- The writer uses specific details to make a clear picture for the reader.

Conrad helps the reader "see" the open cupboard door. He uses details to help me know what is inside.

> That big yellow box, just inside the door

Organization

- The poem's form or shape makes the ideas clear for the reader.

Conrad changes line lengths at the end of each stanza. The poem has its own special form or shape.

Holds more...
JUICE!

Voice

- The voice is original and enthusiastic.

Voice is the way writing sounds. The last lines of each stanza sound as if Conrad is talking to me. I can almost hear his voice.

That big yellow box, just inside the door
Holds more...
NOODLES!

Word Choice

- The words chosen for the poem are strong and clear.

Conrad describes one bottle using the words *tall* and *cold*. They help us know what the bottle looks like and feels like.

> That tall, cold bottle, just inside the door

Sentence Fluency

- The poem sounds natural and smooth.
- It is easy to read.

The poem has a good beat. Lots of words are repeated. Some words rhyme. This makes the poem easy to read.

> Big box, little box, which holds more?
> That big yellow box, just inside the door
> Holds more…

Conventions

- Sentences use adjectives and adverbs correctly to create meaning.

I read the poem again. Conrad uses adjectives and adverbs correctly. Here is an example.

Tall bottle, short bottle, which holds more?

Presentation The poem is neat and legible.

My Turn!

Now it's my turn. I'm going to write my own poem. Read on to see how I will do it.

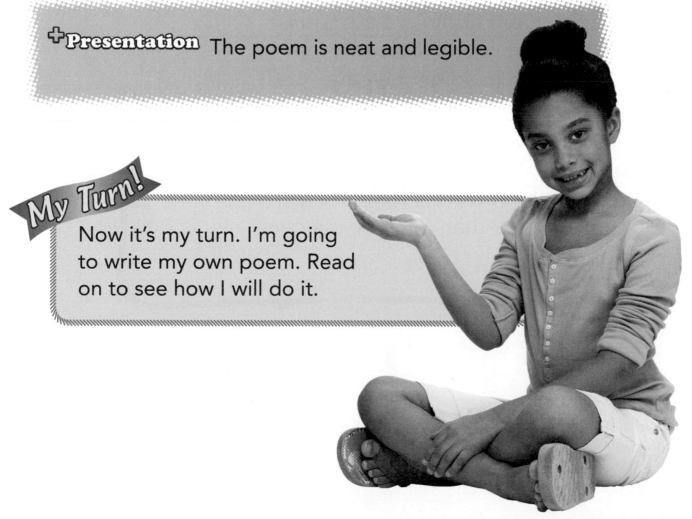

Prewrite

Focus on **Ideas**

The Rubric Says The writer uses specific details to make a clear picture for the reader.

Writing Strategy Use the best details for the poem.

My teacher has asked us to write a poem about a math topic. First, I must pick a topic that I can explain to someone else. Then, I will make a list of topics. I'll write some notes about each one. The notes will help me to pick the best topic. I'll circle my choice. After that, I'll write my own poem.

Math Topics	My Notes
two-digit addition	Adding two-digit numbers is hard for me. I want to choose something I do better.
fact families	I like fact families, but I think it might be hard to explain them in a poem.
add or subtract	It would be fun to write about word problems. I could write questions about animals!

Reflect

Read Alisha's notes. Which topic would you choose? Why?

Apply

Make a list of topics. Write notes about each one.

Prewrite

Focus on **Organization**

The Rubric Says The poem's form or shape makes the ideas clear for the reader.

Writing Strategy Make a Web to organize the poem.

I already know how to write a poem with four lines. The four lines can be one stanza. I have room on my page to write three different stanzas. I will make a Web with three boxes. Each box can describe a different stanza in my poem.

Writer's Term

Web

A **Web** shows details or events. The topic goes in the center box. The details go in the outside boxes.

First Stanza:
Yellow birds singing
(addition)

Second Stanza:
Gray ducks swimming
(subtraction)

Topic

Addition and Subtraction

Third Stanza:
Owls hooting
(surprise)

Reflect

Does the Web give the topic for each stanza? Does it tell which math topic will be covered?

Apply

Make your own Web. Use this page as a model.

Draft

Focus on **Voice**

The Rubric Says The voice is original and enthusiastic.

Writing Strategy Write a catchy title.

I will use my Web and the rubric to help me write my draft. The rubric tells me to use an original and enthusiastic voice. One way to do this is to write a catchy title. A catchy title makes readers want to read the poem. If the title is a question, the readers will want to find out the answer.

Writer's Term

Voice

Voice is the way writing sounds. Voice can be silly, serious, or sad. A title can help show the writer's voice.

Proofreading Marks

/ Make a small letter
∧ Add something
ℓ Take out something
⊙ Add a period
≡ Make a capital letter

[DRAFT]

How Many Birds?
by Alisha

catchy title

Twelve yellow birds
Sing sweetly in a tree.
If more join them,
How many sing for me?

Eight gray ducks
swim quiet in the rain.
Some ducks fly away.
How many ducks remain?

Seven brown owls hoot at the
midnight moon.
Owls sleep during the day.
So how many hoot at noon?

Reflect

What do you think of Alisha's title?

Apply

Write your first draft. Include a title.

Revise

Focus on **Word Choice**

The Rubric Says The words chosen for the poem are strong and clear.

Writing Strategy Replace weak adjectives with strong ones.

A poem does not have many words. Every word I choose has to be the best word for the job.

I found the word *brown* in the third stanza. It does not tell as much about owls as I would like. When I think of owls, I think of their puffy feathers. I will change the word *brown* to *feathery*. It is a stronger adjective.

Writer's Term

Adjectives

An **adjective** is a word that describes a noun. A noun is a person, place, or thing. An adjective usually goes before the noun it tells about.

[DRAFT]

How Many Birds?
by Alisha

Twelve yellow birds
Sing sweetly in a tree.
If more join them,
How many sing for me?

Eight gray ducks
swim quiet in the rain.
Some ducks fly away.
How many ducks remain?

used a strong adjective

Seven ~~brown~~ feathery owls hoot
at the midnight moon.
Owls sleep during the day,
So how many hoot at noon?

Reflect

Look at the adjective Alisha added. Do you think that it is a stronger adjective?

Apply

Now look at your draft. Add a title to show your voice.

Revise

Focus on **Sentence Fluency**

The Rubric Says The poem sounds natural and smooth. It is easy to read.

Writing Strategy Read aloud the poem.

Remember that poems do not always have sentences. They have lines. The lines need to be smooth and easy to read. If the lines sound choppy or rambling, I need to change some words to smooth them out. If I read my poem aloud, I can tell where the lines are hard to read.

[DRAFT]

Seven brown owls hoot ~~at the~~
~~midnight moon~~.
At the midnight moon.
Owls sleep ^ during the day,
So how many hoot at noon?

made two lines out of one

Reflect

Did Alisha follow the rubric? Do any of the lines sound like they don't fit in the poem? Which lines needed to be smoothed out?

Apply

Look at your draft. Check to see if you have written any awkward lines. If so, smooth them out so they fit the beat of the poem.

Edit

Focus on **Conventions**

The Rubric Says Sentences use adjectives and adverbs correctly to create meaning.

Writing Strategy Use adjectives and adverbs correctly.

The rubric says to check the use of adjectives and adverbs. If they are not used correctly, my readers could become confused.

I will also check to make sure my spelling and punctuation are correct. Every sentence should begin with a capital letter. Every sentence should end with a period, a question mark, or an exclamation point.

Writer's Term

Adjectives and Adverbs

An **adjective** describes a noun. An **adverb** describes a verb. They answer how, where, or when questions. Adverbs that tell how often end in **-ly**.

[DRAFT]

Eight gray ducks
Swim quietly in the rain.
~~Some~~ Three ducks fly away.
How many ducks remain?

fixed an adverb

capitalized a word

Reflect

A poem may have lines and sentences. If a sentence asks a question, how should it end?

Apply

Check all adverbs. If an adverb tells how, it may end in **-ly**. Capitalize the first word in each line of a poem. Use punctuation correctly.

Comparing With Adjectives

Know the Rule

An **adjective** can describe by comparing two people, places, or things. Add *-er* to some adjectives to compare two things.

Example: An eagle flies **higher** than a songbird.

An adjective can also compare more than two people, places, or things. Add *-est* to some adjectives to compare more than two things.

Example: The **fastest** horse won the race.

Practice the Rule

Number a separate sheet of paper 1–5. Write each sentence. Circle the correct form of the adjective.

1. A horse is (taller/tallest) than a pig.
2. Who ran (faster/fastest), Jason or Belinda?
3. Is a turtle's shell (smaller/smallest) than a snail's shell?
4. Lucy is the (sweeter/sweetest) dog we've ever had.
5. Sam thinks that subtracting is (harder/hardest) than adding.

Adjectives and Adverbs

Know the Rule

An **adjective** tells about a noun.

Example: My dog has **black** ears and **white** paws.

An **adverb** tells about a verb. It tells how, when, or where something is done. In this example, the adverb tells how the dog barks.

Example: My dog barks **loudly**.

Practice the Rule

Number a separate sheet of paper 1–6. Write the adjective or adverb that makes sense in each sentence.

1. The kitten has (soft/softly) fur.
2. The birds sing (sweet/sweetly) in the trees.
3. The (bright/brightly) sun made me blink.
4. The mice ran (quick/quickly) away from the cat.
5. Play (quiet/quietly) so you won't wake the baby.
6. Dolphins swim (smooth/smoothly).

Publish

+Presentation

Publishing Strategy Make a recording of your poem.

Presentation Strategy Use your best handwriting or word processing.

First, I will use my best handwriting or word processing to copy my poem. This will make it easy to read. Then, we will all record our poems. We will do a podcast. We will play our poems for our families and friends.

My Final Checklist

Did I —

✔ correct any mistakes?

✔ use my best handwriting?

✔ read with my best voice?

FINAL DRAFT

How Many Birds?
by Alisha

Twelve yellow birds
Sing sweetly in a tree.
If four more join them,
How many sing for me?

Eight gray ducks
Swim quietly in the rain.
Three ducks fly away.
How many ducks remain?

Seven feathery owls
Hoot at the midnight moon.
Owls sleep during the day,
So how many hoot at noon?

Apply

How did Alisha do? Be sure to use the rubric to check your final draft.

Descriptive test writing

Read the Writing Prompt

Every writing test starts with a writing prompt. Most writing prompts have three parts:

Setup This tells what you need to know to get ready for writing.

Task This tells exactly what you're supposed to write.

Scoring Guide This part tells how your writing will be scored. If you do everything on the list, you should do well on the test.

A scoring guide is a lot like a rubric. It lists everything you need to think about to write a good paper. Many scoring guides will have the same parts as the rubrics we've looked at:

- Ideas
- Organization
- Voice
- Word Choice
- Sentence Fluency
- Conventions

Writing MODEL Prompt

Is there a person who is very special to you? Do you have a favorite place or a favorite object? Think of a person, place, or thing you know very well.

Write a descriptive paper about a person, place, or thing that is important in your life. Choose a topic that you know very well and want to tell about.

Be sure your descriptive paper

- has a clear topic and interesting details.
- is organized around the five senses.
- uses a personal "you" writer's voice.
- uses clear describing words.
- has long and short sentences.
- has correct capitalization, punctuation, and spelling.

Writing Traits
in the Scoring Guide

The scoring guide on page 389 has been made into this chart. How is it like the rubrics you've been using? Not all test prompts have all six writing traits. This one does!

Ideas	• Be sure your paper has a clear topic and interesting details.
Organization	• Be sure your paper is organized around the five senses.
Voice	• Be sure your paper uses a personal "you" writer's voice.
Word Choice	• Be sure your paper uses clear describing words.
Sentence Fluency	• Be sure your paper has long and short sentences.
Conventions	• Be sure your paper has correct capitalization, punctuation, and spelling.

Look at Justin Chan's paper. Did he follow the scoring guide?

Writing Prompt **MODEL** Response

Our Apple Tree

by Justin Chan

Our apple tree changes through the year. In winter, you can see its dark, rough bark and many branches. In spring it gets white blossoms. Then petals float down, and green leaves come out. You hear birds chirping there.

All summer the apple tree gives cool shade. Later in the summer, you see small green apples. More red shows as they grow.

In fall, the whole tree smells like fruit. You can pick the biggest apple and taste the first sweet juicy bite. Then you fill baskets with apples and save them. The leaves turn yellow. A cold wind will blow them down. The changes through the seasons will begin again.

Using the Scoring Guide to Study the Model

Now let's use the scoring guide to check Justin's writing test, "Our Apple Tree."

Ideas

- The paper has a clear topic and interesting details.

Justin tells his topic clearly at the start of his paper. Then he gives an example with interesting details.

Our apple tree changes through the year. In winter, you can see its dark, rough bark and many branches.

Organization

- The paper is organized around the five senses.

Justin describes the apple tree in winter, spring, summer, and fall. He uses at least one of the senses for each season. He uses all five senses in the paper. Which senses does he use here?

All summer the apple tree gives cool shade. Later in the summer, you see small green apples.

Voice

- The paper uses a personal "you" writer's voice.

By using the word "you," Justin helps me feel that he is talking right to me. He connects "you" with action words so I feel like I am doing things along with him.

You hear birds chirping there.

Using the Scoring Guide to Study the Model

Word Choice

- The paper uses clear describing words.

Justin gives me a clear picture of the apple tree. He tells about it in every season and describes how it changes. Look at his describing words.

Later in the summer, you see small green apples. More red shows as they grow.

Sentence Fluency

- The paper has long and short sentences.

Justin uses both long and short sentences. His shortest sentence has four words. His longest has thirteen. Here is a short sentence followed by a longer one.

In fall, the whole tree smells like fruit. You can pick the biggest apple and taste the first sweet juicy bite.

Conventions

- The capitalization, punctuation, and spelling are correct.

Justin's final draft does not have mistakes. His capitalization and punctuation are correct. I do not see any spelling errors there. Do you see any other kinds of errors?

Many tests are timed. Your teacher will tell you how much time you have to take a test. Look on the next two pages for some tips on how to plan your time and take a test.

Planning My Time

Look at the picture of the clock. Do you see that there is more green than any other color? That means you should spend most of your time getting ready to write. What takes the least amount of time?

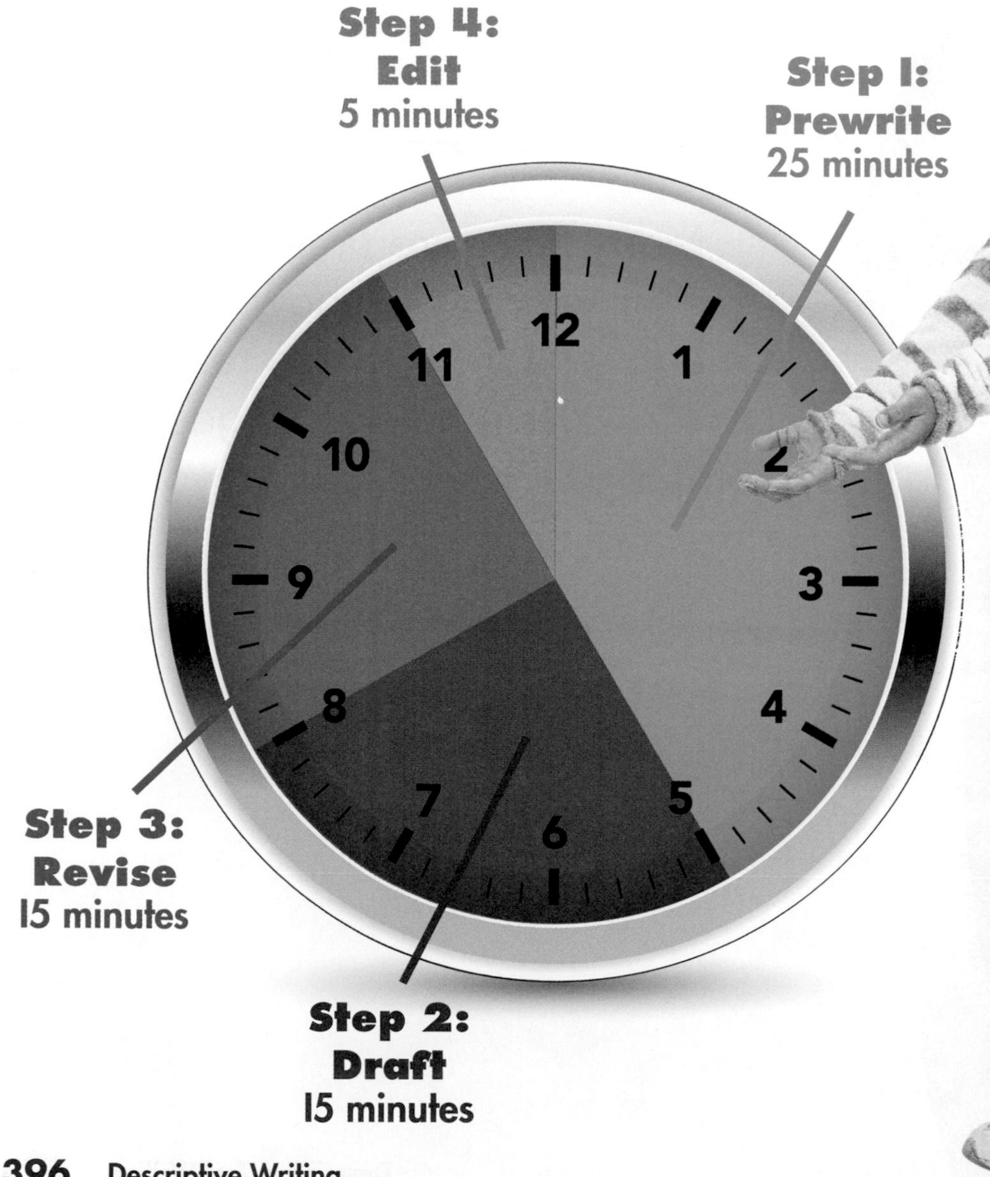

Remember these important tips when you write for a test.

TEST TIPS

1. Study the writing prompt before you start to write.
2. Make sure you understand the task before you start to write.
3. Keep an eye on the clock.
4. Reread your writing. Compare it to the scoring guide at least twice.
5. Plan, plan, plan!
6. Write neatly.

Prewrite

Focus on **Ideas**

Writing Strategy Study the writing prompt and choose a topic.

Getting ready to write is a big step. I started with the prompt. First, I studied the setup. That helped me think of topics.

Next, I looked carefully at the task. That helped me choose from different ideas. One idea was my bunk bed. I just got it, so I don't have a lot to say about it yet.

Another idea was my great set of colored pencils. That is something I know well and use a lot. It is special and I want to tell about it. Now, I am going to write notes about my topic.

My Writing Test Prompt

Setup — Think of a favorite place or a favorite thing. It could be at home or at school. Think of what you know about it. Why is it special to you?

Task — Write a paper about a favorite place or thing. Choose a topic that you know very well. Think of how you will describe it. Tell why it is special.

Here are my notes about my colored pencils.

Notes

- got them with a gift card in art store
- for my birthday last year
- box has slots for sixteen pencils
- love to write and draw with them
- better than crayons

Apply

Read the setup and the task carefully. Choose your best topic. Then make notes to help you write about your topic.

Prewrite

Focus on Organization

Writing Strategy Make a graphic organizer.

I wrote some notes about my topic. Now I can take the next step. I just read the scoring guide. It says to use the five senses. I will fill in a Five-Senses Chart.

That chart is good for a descriptive paper. It will give me more ways to describe my pencils. Charts help me get organized.

Graphic Organizer: Five-Senses Chart

Topic: My Colored Pencils

I can **see**	• sixteen colors, but make more by mixing them • in a row, like a rainbow	• lines and designs • shapes fill the paper as I use more pencils
I can **hear**	• sound of pencils rolling in the box • clinking on desk	• soft sound of drawing on smooth paper
I can **taste**	• not good to eat or chew on pencils	• imagine taste of foods I draw, such as fruits and carrots
I can **touch** (feel)	• smooth, slim, shiny, strong • moves like roller skates on paper	• press hard for thick, bright color
I can **smell**	• nice, spicy smell when I open the box	• wood smell when I sharpen

Reflect

Look at the words Alisha has put into the chart. Which one of the senses might be hard with her topic?

Apply

How can you use the five senses for your topic? Fill in your own chart.

Draft

Focus on **Ideas**

Writing Strategy Describe the topic clearly.

A descriptive paper should have a clear topic. The topic is my colored pencils. I will tell that at the start. Then I will keep writing about the topic.

I have good details about the pencils from my notes and my chart. I will try to use the details in my draft.

I will check the scoring guide as I write. I plan to follow all of the six traits. If I do that, I should do well on the test.

Proofreading Marks

/ Make a small letter

∧ Add something

ℓ Take out something

⊙ Add a period

≡ Make a capital letter

[DRAFT]

My Colored Pencils

clear topic

I love my colored pencils. This is why. I got them with a gift card in an art store. I chose the box of sixten shiny pencils.

The colored pencils are much better than crayons. I can make thin lines. I can make neat letters. I make cards pictures and sines.

I like the sound of pencils. I like the smell of wood when I sharpen my pencils. I love when I write or draw.

Reflect

Read Alisha's draft. What is her topic? Has she made it clear to you?

Apply

Make sure to describe your topic clearly in your draft.

Revise

Focus on Ideas

Writing Strategy Add details to support the topic.

I just read my draft. I think it needs more interesting details about my topic. I found some in my notes and my chart. Those words will help me explain why I chose the colored pencils.

I see where I can add some words. Then readers will understand why I love these pencils.

There is not much time to revise. I will do that now.

[DRAFT]

I love my colored pencils. This is why. I got them with a gift card in an art store on my Birthday. I chose the box of sixten shiny pencils like a rainbow.

The colored pencils are much better than crayons. I can make thin lines. I can make neat letters. I make cards pictures and sines.

added interesting details

Reflect

What words has Alisha added? Do they help you understand why she loves her colored pencils?

Apply

Read your own draft. Where can you add interesting details? Will they support your topic?

Revise

Focus on Organization

Writing Strategy Use words from the Five-Senses Chart.

The scoring guide says to use the five senses. I have used three senses in the draft. One was what I hear, but there are better describing words for that in the chart.

Also, I want to use words for touch. That helps tell why I love to use my pencils.

For this test, I won't have time to explain about the sense of taste.

[DRAFT]

The colored pencils are much better than crayons. I can make thin lines. I can make neat letters. I make cards pictures and sines.

I like the clinking sound of pencils. I like the smell of wood when I sharpen my pencils. I love their smooth feel when I write or draw.

added senses

Reflect

Which senses did Alisha add this time? What did you find out about her colored pencils?

Apply

Check off the senses you have used in your draft. Can you add other senses? Can you add better words?

Edit

Focus on Conventions

Writing Strategy Check the capitalization, punctuation, and spelling.

My last step is to edit the draft. First, I need to check my sentences. Each one should start with a capital letter. Also, I want to make sure that I put commas where they belong.

Next, I will check my spelling. My teacher told me to touch each word with my pencil. That helps me look at each word carefully.

Then my test will be done!

FINAL DRAFT

corrected capitalization

My Colored Pencils

by Alisha

I love my colored pencils~~.~~, and I will tell you ~~This is~~ why. I got them with a gift card in an art store on my ~~B~~irthday. I chose the box of sixteen shiny pencils like a rainbow.

The colored pencils are much better than crayons. I can make thin lines~~. I can make~~ and neat letters. you can see them in my ~~I make~~ cards, pictures, and si~~nes~~gns.

corrected spelling

corrected punctuation

I like the clinking sound of pencils on my desk. I like the smell of wood when I sharpen my pencils. I love their smooth feel when I write or draw.

Reflect

Check Alisha's paper against the scoring guide. Then check your own paper.

Appendix A
Grammar Practice

Subjects and Predicates

Know the Rule

The **subject** of a sentence tells who or what did or does something.

Example: Alonzo watched the horse.

The **predicate** of a sentence tells what the subject did or does.

Example: The horse **ran** fast.

Practice the Rule

Number a sheet of paper 1–6. Next to each number, write the underlined word and label it **subject** or **predicate**.

1. The <u>dog</u> scared the horse.
2. The <u>horse</u> stopped.
3. Cesar <u>won</u> the race.
4. <u>Eduardo</u> rode three miles.
5. Kaya <u>loves</u> her horse.
6. I <u>ride</u> my horse every day.

Telling Sentences and Asking Sentences

Know the Rule

A **telling sentence** makes a statement. It ends with a period.

Example: The ball rolled across the floor.

An **asking sentence** asks a question. It ends with a question mark.

Example: Can you find the ball?

Practice the Rule

Number a sheet of paper 1–6. Next to each number, write **telling sentence** or **asking sentence**.

1. Do you like baseball?
2. Emilio loves baseball.
3. Do you know the rules?
4. Will you join the team?
5. When does the game start?
6. Jason is the pitcher.

Sentences That Show Strong Feelings

Know the Rule

A **sentence that shows strong feelings,** such as excitement, surprise, or fear, usually ends with an exclamation point. It begins with a capital letter.

Example: We can't wait to start**!**

Practice the Rule

Number a sheet of paper 1–6. Next to each number, write **asking sentence** if the sentence asks a question. Write **strong feelings** if the sentence shows strong feelings.

1. What is that animal?
2. Is it a cat?
3. I think it is a skunk!
4. Are skunks black?
5. Do they have a white stripe?
6. We have to get away!

Prepositional Phrases

Know the Rule

A **prepositional phrase** adds information to a sentence.

Prepositional Phrases		
to the park	of treats	on the ground
in the air	in the yard	under the table
to me	of toys	on the table

Practice the Rule

Number a sheet of paper 1–6. Choose a prepositional phrase from the box to complete each sentence. Write the sentences.

1. My dog jumps high ____.
2. He finds the ball ____.
3. I buy him bags ____.
4. I place the ball ____.
5. My dog is ____.
6. He has a lot ____.

Compound Sentences

Know the Rule

A **compound sentence** tells two complete thoughts. The two parts of a compound sentence are joined by a comma and the word *and*, *but*, or *or*.

Example: Dad made soup, **but** I was not hungry.

Practice the Rule

Number a sheet of paper 1–8. Use the word **and, but,** or **or** to join the sentences. Write the sentences.

1. I like meatloaf, ____ my brother likes chicken.
2. I made a salad, ____ my aunt made a cake.
3. We could eat supper now, ____ we could wait.
4. Supper was good, ____ everyone loved it.
5. I washed the dishes, ____ my sister put them away.
6. We played games, ____ everyone had fun.
7. I tried hard, ____ I did not win.
8. We were tired, ____ we went to bed.

Sentence Fragments

Know the Rule

A **sentence** must have a naming part (subject) and an action part (predicate). If a sentence is missing either part, it is called a **sentence fragment**.

Examples: Swam in the lake. *(missing the subject)*
My friend and I. *(missing the predicate)*

Practice the Rule

Number a sheet of paper 1–8. Fix the sentence fragments by making them sentences. Write the sentences.

1. Slept in a tent.
2. Went fishing.
3. Had a picnic.
4. The sky.
5. My father.
6. Loved the water.
7. Grilled our food.
8. Went home on Saturday.

Nouns

Know the Rule

A **noun** names a person, animal, place, or thing.

Examples: Alicia **Detroit**
lion **hat**

Practice the Rule

Number a sheet of paper 1–8. Copy the sentences. Underline the nouns.

1. The car was in the driveway.
2. Sofia filled the bucket.
3. Carlos added soap.
4. Nori cleaned the windows.
5. Oki worked hard.
6. Carlos rinsed the car.
7. Mim brought the towels.
8. The car looked great.

Plural Nouns

Know the Rule

A **singular noun** names one person, animal, place, or thing. A **plural noun** names more than one person, animal, place, or thing. Many plural nouns are formed by adding *-s* to the end of a singular noun.

Example: apples

Add *-es* to nouns that end in *x, ch, s,* or *sh*.

Examples: peaches
bushes

Practice the Rule

Number a sheet of paper 1–10. Write the correct plural form of each noun.

1. runner
2. class
3. girl
4. fox
5. inch
6. book
7. worker
8. dish
9. box
10. pet

Common Nouns and Proper Nouns

Know the Rule

A **common noun** names any person, place, or thing. A **proper noun** names a certain person, place, or thing. A proper noun begins with a capital letter.

Examples: city *(common)* **Chicago** *(proper)*
store *(common)* **Jake's Books** *(proper)*

Practice the Rule

Number a sheet of paper 1–8. Write **common** or **proper** to describe each underlined noun.

1. Marta is my best friend.
2. Marta moved to Phoenix last year.
3. Lin lives on Elm Street.
4. Julio goes to Hamilton Elementary School.
5. Marta wrote me a letter on Sunday.
6. Julio has a new dog.
7. Valentine's Day is in February.
8. Peru is a country.

Personal Pronouns

Know the Rule

A **pronoun** takes the place of a noun. Make sure a pronoun agrees with the noun it replaces. Singular pronouns are *I, you, he, she,* and *it*. Plural pronouns are *we, you,* and *they*.

Examples:
Ali plays soccer. **He** plays soccer.
Pedro and Jack like soccer. **They** like soccer.

Practice the Rule

Number a sheet of paper 1–6. Replace the underlined noun or nouns with the correct personal pronoun. Write the sentences.

1. <u>Holly and Jorge</u> made the poster.
2. <u>Jorge</u> thought of the idea.
3. <u>Holly</u> drew the pictures.
4. <u>The judges</u> liked the poster.
5. <u>The poster</u> won first prize.
6. Tomorrow, <u>Nina</u> will give a report.

Possessive Pronouns

Know the Rule

A **possessive pronoun** shows ownership. Singular possessive pronouns are *my, your, his, her,* and *its.* Plural possessive pronouns are *our, your,* and *their.*

Examples: His cat ran away.
Their horse won first prize.

Practice the Rule

Number a sheet of paper 1–8. Write the sentences. Underline the possessive pronouns.

1. My horse runs races.
2. His name is Beacon.
3. Beacon is my best friend.
4. Our friendship is important.
5. My job is to take care of Beacon.
6. Sometimes my parents help.
7. I am glad to have their help.
8. My brother has a horse, too.

Using *I* and *Me*

Know the Rule

Use **I** or **me** to talk about yourself. Use **I** as the subject of the sentence. Use **me** after action verbs or words such as *for, to, with,* and *at.*

Examples: I practice every day. My father helps **me**.

When you talk about yourself and another person, always name the other person first.

Example: Brian and **I** practice together.

Practice the Rule

Number a sheet of paper 1–6. Choose the correct pronoun to complete the sentences. Write the sentences.

1. I will take a camera with (I/me).
2. Kim and (I/me) are best friends.
3. Kim gave (I/me) a new book.
4. Michiko beat (I/me) in the race.
5. Michiko and (I/me) will race next week.
6. Michiko loves racing against (I/me).

Adjectives

Know the Rule

An **adjective** tells more about a noun.

Adjectives			
smart	smelly	loud	wet
silver	colorful	old	black

Practice the Rule

Number a sheet of paper 1–8. Choose an adjective to complete each sentence. Write the sentences.

1. The ____ parrot talks.
2. The ____ fish swims fast.
3. The ____ dog sleeps a lot.
4. A ____ bark woke us up.
5. The ____ kitten is cute.
6. We gave the ____ dog a bath.
7. Now his fur is ____.
8. The ____ dog knows lots of tricks.

Action Verbs

Know the Rule

An **action verb** tells what someone or something did or does.

Examples: Mia **runs** down the road.
The wind **blows**.

Practice the Rule

Number a sheet of paper 1–8. Write each sentence. Draw a line under the action verb.

1. We swim in the lake.
2. Birds fly by.
3. Pam jumps rope.
4. Jason walks to the car.
5. A strong wind blows.
6. Carlos builds a sand castle.
7. One boat sails on the river.
8. We ride our bikes.

More Action Verbs

Know the Rule

Use strong **action verbs** to help you write better sentences. A strong action verb gives you the best idea about what is happening.

Practice the Rule

Number a sheet of paper 1–8. Write each sentence. Choose the strongest action verb to complete the sentence.

1. Ted (races/goes) to the finish line.
2. Ari (hits/smashes) the ball.
3. The horse (moves/runs) fast.
4. The frogs (leap/go) over each other.
5. Ricardo (does/scrubs) the counter.
6. Marcus (eats/has) the food.
7. Huge waves (crash/go) over the rocks.
8. Seaweed (goes/floats) by.

Present Tense and Past Tense

Know the Rule

Present-tense verbs show that an action happens now. **Past-tense verbs** show that an action happened in the past. Add *-ed* to show the past tense of most verbs. Some past-tense verbs have a different form.

Present		Past	
walk	sits	walked	sat
hides	tells	hid	told

Practice the Rule

Number a sheet of paper 1–6. Look at the underlined verbs. Name the verb tense. Beside each number, write **present** or **past**.

1. Ben watched Lei dance.
2. Juan runs fast.
3. Brian fixes his drawing.
4. My dad told me a story.
5. Yesterday, we visited a ranch.
6. It rained in the afternoon.

Helping Verbs

Know the Rule

Helping verbs come before the main verb in a sentence. Some helping verbs are **am, is, are, was, were, will, has, have,** and **had**.

Example: Anya **is** learning to dance.

Practice the Rule

Number a sheet of paper 1–8. Write the sentences. Underline the helping verb. Circle the main verb.

1. Sam will race in the wheelchair race.
2. He has trained for months.
3. He has lifted weights.
4. Sam has worked hard.
5. My parents are coming to the race.
6. They will watch Sam's race.
7. Racers will use special wheelchairs.
8. The race will begin at 9:00 A.M.

Adverbs

Know the Rule

An **adverb** tells more about a verb. Adverbs tell how, when, or where. They often end with *-ly*.

How	When	Where
carefully	often	inside
brightly	always	there
quickly	once	upstairs

Practice the Rule

Number a sheet of paper 1–6. Choose an adverb to complete each sentence. Write the sentences.

1. We ____ have picnics.
2. My brother ____ sets the table.
3. The napkins are ____.
4. The sun shone ____.
5. ____ it rained.
6. We had to take the food ____.

Prepositions of Place

Know the Rule

A **preposition** shows how words are connected with other words in a sentence. Some prepositions show where an object or person is.

Prepositions		
around	by	near
before	in	on
behind	into	under

Practice the Rule

Number a sheet of paper 1–6. Choose the preposition that best completes each sentence. Write the sentences.

1. I planted my garden ____ the front yard.
2. My garden is ____ the window.
3. The watering can is ____ the stairs.
4. I put a small fence ____ the garden.
5. ____ the garden is a brick wall.
6. There is an apple tree ____ the street.

Conjunctions

Know the Rule

Conjunctions are words that join words or groups of words. *And, but,* and *or* are conjunctions.

Example: Melissa **and** Jose gave a report on birds.

Practice the Rule

Number a sheet of paper 1–8. Write each sentence. Underline the conjunctions.

1. Most parrots live in wild places, but some live in zoos.
2. Macaws and lovebirds are two kinds of parrots.
3. There are many parrots in Australia and Central America.
4. Parrots eat fruit, flowers, and nuts.
5. Their beaks and feet help them climb.
6. Many people buy and keep parrots as pets.
7. My uncle and aunt have parrots.
8. I would like to have a parrot or a canary as a pet.

Its and It's

Know the Rule

Its means "belonging to." **Its** is often confused with **it's**. **It's** is a shortened way of saying "it is."

Examples: The dog wagged **its** tail.
It's hot today.

Practice the Rule

Number a sheet of paper 1–8. Write the sentences. Complete each sentence by writing **its** or **it's**.

1. ____ time for us to go.
2. Make sure the fish eats ____ food.
3. The dog lost ____ collar.
4. ____ under the couch.
5. The dog is eating ____ dinner.
6. I think ____ going to rain.
7. ____ fun to go to the park.
8. ____ going to be a great day.

Irregular Verbs

Know the Rule

Verbs that do not add *-ed* to show the past tense are called **irregular verbs**.

Present	Past
is	was
give	gave
see	saw

Practice the Rule

Number a sheet of paper 1–6. Write each sentence. Complete the sentence with the past tense of the verb.

1. The coach ____ us uniforms. (give)
2. My uniform ____ too big. (is)
3. I ____ my parents in the stands. (see)
4. My father ____ waving. (is)
5. My family ____ me get a hit. (see)
6. After the game, the coach ____ everyone a medal. (give)

Compound Words

Know the Rule

A **compound word** is made up of two words.

Compound Words			
lighthouse	laptop	baseball	pancakes
nightlight	sidewalk	briefcase	outside

Practice the Rule

Number a sheet of paper 1–8. Find a compound word to complete each sentence. Write the sentences.

1. I found a penny on the ____.
2. It is raining ____.
3. Do you like to play ____?
4. A ____ guides ships.
5. I have a ____ in my room.
6. Grandma made ____ for breakfast.
7. Dad works on a ____.
8. Mom carries a ____ to work.

Subject-Verb Agreement

Know the Rule

In a sentence, the **subject** and the **verb** must **agree**. If the subject is singular, the verb must be singular. If the subject is plural, the verb must be plural. Collective nouns, such as *class*, tell about more than one person. But use a singular noun with them.

Examples: **Tyler is** leaning about animals.
We are learning about animals.
Our **class is** learning about animals.

Practice the Rule

Number a sheet of paper 1–6. Choose the verb that best completes the sentence. Write the sentences.

1. Min (collect/collects) facts about animals.
2. Min's family (see/sees) bats in the evening.
3. Texas (has/have) many kinds of bats.
4. Nick (play/plays) on a baseball team.
5. The team (is/are) called the Ravens.
6. The whole class (cheer/cheers) for the team!

Comparing With Adjectives

Know the Rule

An **adjective** can describe by comparing two people, places, or things. Add *-er* to adjectives to compare two people, places, or things.

Example: Binh is tall. Binh is **taller** than Clara.

An **adjective** can also compare more than two people, places, or things. Add *-est* to adjectives to compare more than two people, places, or things.

Example: Binh is the **tallest** person in our class.

Practice the Rule

Number a sheet of paper 1–6. Choose the adjective that best completes the sentence. Write the sentence.

1. Leslie runs (faster/fastest) than Juan.
2. In our class, Pete runs the (faster/fastest).
3. I am (older/oldest) than my sister.
4. The (older/oldest) person in the room is my grandmother.
5. Your sandwich is (larger/largest) than mine.
6. I got the (smaller/smallest) sandwich of all.

Abbreviations

Know the Rule

An **abbreviation** is a short form of a word. An abbreviation begins with a capital letter and ends with a period.

Months	Mar. (March)	Apr. (April)	Sept. (September)
Days	Mon. (Monday)	Thurs. (Thursday)	Fri. (Friday)
Titles	Mr. (Mister)	Dr. (Doctor)	Jr. (Junior)
Addresses	Rd. (Road)	St. (Street)	Ave. (Avenue)

Practice the Rule

Number a sheet of paper 1–8. Write the words. Beside each word write the correct abbreviation.

1. Mister
2. April
3. Street
4. Monday
5. Road
6. Avenue
7. September
8. Friday

Contractions

Know the Rule

A **contraction** is a short way of writing and saying two words. An apostrophe (') shows where letters were left out.

Examples:

doesn't	(does not)	haven't	(have not)
wasn't	(was not)	can't	(cannot)
don't	(do not)		

Practice the Rule

Number a sheet of paper 1–6. Write each sentence. Replace the underlined words with the correct contraction.

1. <u>Do not</u> leave your room a mess.
2. It <u>was not</u> clean yesterday.
3. I <u>cannot</u> find your glasses.
4. Your room <u>does not</u> look clean.
5. I <u>have not</u> cleaned it yet.
6. You <u>have not</u> swept the floor.

Commas in a Series

Know the Rule

A **series** is a list of three or more words or phrases. Use **commas** to separate these words or phrases. The last comma goes before *and* or *or*.

Example: We ate chicken, salad, **and** beans.

Practice the Rule

Number a sheet of paper 1–8. Write each sentence. Add commas where they are needed.

1. We grew beans, potatoes and beets.
2. I like milk juice and water.
3. We played baseball football and soccer.
4. The weather was windy rainy and cold.
5. I brought sandwiches, water and napkins.
6. Ralph, Julie and Maya played the best.
7. My favorite animals are whales dogs and cats.
8. We saw rivers mountains, and lakes.

Commas in Dates

Know the Rule

When you write a **date,** put a **comma** between the day and the year, like this: May 10, 2012.

Practice the Rule

Number a sheet of paper 1–5. Write each date. Add commas where they are needed.

1. June 24 1997
2. May 16 2013
3. June 6 1999
4. December 8 2012
5. August 9 2011

Add the numbers 6–8. Write a date to answer each question.

6. When were you born?
7. What is today's date?
8. What is yesterday's date?

Parts of a Friendly Letter

Know the Rule

A friendly letter has five parts:

1. The **heading** has the writer's address and the date.
2. The **greeting** begins with **Dear** followed by the name of the person you are writing. Put a comma after the greeting.
3. The **body** tells the message.
4. The **closing** comes at the end of the letter. It might say, **Your Friend** or **Sincerely**. Put a comma after your closing.
5. The **signature** is where you sign your name. The signatures comes right below the closing.

Practice the Rule

Number a sheet of paper 1–5. Write the part of the letter.

15 West Street
(1) Houston, Texas 77003
July 20, 2012

Dear Camila, (2)

We are at Key Largo in Florida. You would love it here. We went to the state park. I went fishing. It was a fun day.
(3) I can't wait to see you when we get home.

(4) Your Friend,
(5) Carla

Quotation Marks

Know the Rule

Use **quotation marks** at the beginning and at the end of a speaker's exact words. When you write the exact words a speaker says, you are writing a **direct quotation**.

Examples: "Wait for me," Marcia said.
Mr. Springer said, "Today we will learn about fables."

Practice the Rule

Number a sheet of paper 1–6. Write the sentences. Put quotation marks before and after direct quotations.

1. I am going to win this contest, Marisa said.
2. Juan said, You did a really good job on your poster.
3. I hope Marisa wins, Miguel said.
4. I like her poster on tigers, Nori said.
5. I hope the judges like my work, Marisa said.
6. The contest is tomorrow, Sarah said.

Book Titles

Know the Rule

Capitalize the first word, the last word, and all important words in **book titles**. Underline a book title when you write it. Use *italics* on the computer.

Examples: The Cat in the Hat *The Cat in the Hat*

Practice the Rule

Number a sheet of paper 1–8. Write the titles correctly.

1. the Adventures of taxi dog
2. Nim's island
3. sneakers, the seaside cat
4. dear Max
5. Frog and toad together
6. We Are best friends
7. once Upon a time
8. a Fine, fine school

More Practice

Subject and Predicate

Write the subject and the predicate of each sentence.

1. Janine finished her project.
2. The class liked it.
3. She made posters.
4. Frank asked questions.
5. Janine gave answers.

Telling Sentences and Asking Sentences

If the sentence is a telling sentence, write **telling sentence**.
If the sentence asks a question, write **asking sentence**.

1. What is your favorite class?
2. I like science best.
3. What do you like about science?
4. I like learning about animals.
5. What is your favorite animal?

More Practice

Sentences That Show Strong Feelings

If the sentence asks a question, write **asking sentence**. If it shows strong feelings, write **strong feelings**.

1. Watch out for the flying branch!
2. Where is the dog?
3. Can he hear us calling?
4. Get in the house right now!
5. A hurricane is coming!

Prepositional Phrases

Write each prepositional phrase.

1. The book is on the table.
2. Put it on the desk.
3. The pencil is in my bag.
4. Put the box under the chair.
5. The chair is on the floor.

More Practice

Compound Sentences

Underline the two sentences. Circle the word that joins the sentences.

1. I wrote the report, and Dana made the poster.
2. We studied tigers, and we drew pictures.
3. I liked learning about tigers, but I did not like writing about them.
4. Our report was good, but Carlos gave a better report.
5. Carlos gave a report on lions, and Charlie made a poster.

Sentence Fragments

Write **yes** if the words are a complete sentence. Write **no** if the words are not a complete sentence.

1. Beside the house.
2. I dropped the book.
3. In the middle of the day.
4. Rain began to fall.
5. When I woke up.

More Practice

Nouns

Write the sentences. Underline the nouns.

1. The sunset was beautiful.
2. The sun lit up the mountains.
3. My uncle cooked supper.
4. The food tasted good.
5. My aunt made dessert.

Plural Nouns

Write the correct plural noun of each singular noun.

1. cat
2. peach
3. toolbox
4. sandwich
5. fox

More Practice

Common Nouns and Proper Nouns

Write the sentences. Underline the proper nouns. Circle the common nouns.

1. Pablo plays baseball.
2. The team played a game at Humana Field.
3. Marcia was hit by a pitch on Wednesday.
4. Marcia had to go to Western Hospital.
5. Her team won the game on Friday.

Personal Pronouns

Replace the underlined noun or group of nouns with the correct personal pronoun.

1. Manuel and Felipe are great athletes.
2. Mary plays soccer.
3. Mr. Alvarez makes players play hard.
4. Alicia and Dana play baseball.
5. Mrs. Reynolds is a fun coach to play for.

More Practice

Possessive Pronouns

Write the possessive pronouns in each sentence.

1. I love my computer games.
2. My mother sometimes makes me stop.
3. We have many games in our playroom.
4. Your playroom is cool, too.
5. Your father buys computer games.

Using *I* and *Me*

Write the correct pronoun, either **I** or **me**.

1. Kim and ____ will come to the party.
2. I will bring a present with ____.
3. Mom drove Kim and ____ to the party.
4. ____ liked the party.
5. I brought a goodie bag home with ____.

More Practice

Adjectives

Write the sentences. Underline the adjectives. Circle the noun the adjective tells more about.

1. The beautiful flower bloomed yesterday.
2. It has blue and white petals.
3. I love colorful flowers.
4. Dry flowers need water.
5. Put the flowers in the glass vase.

Action Verbs

Write the sentences. Underline the verb.

1. The dog barks at the mailman.
2. The mailman delivers letters.
3. She puts the letters in the mailbox.
4. My mother reads the mail.
5. My father pays each bill.

More Practice

More Action Verbs

Write the sentences. Use the strongest verb to complete the sentence.

1. The bird (soars/moves) over the trees.
2. Eliana (walks/leaps) for the ball.
3. Maria (has/slurps) her drink.
4. Pablo (paints/does) his poster.
5. The chipmunk (runs/scurries) across the yard.

Present Tense and Past Tense

Write each sentence with the correct present-tense verb.

1. Sometimes Carl (miss) the ball.
2. Nicky always (make) mistakes.
3. Jack (finish) his homework.

Write each sentence with the correct past-tense verb.

4. Gary (walk) to the library.
5. I (play) in the band.

More Practice

Helping Verbs

Write the sentences. Underline the helping verb.

1. Kara is finishing a painting.
2. She has spent hours on it.
3. Her classmates will see it on Thursday.
4. Kara has loved her art classes.
5. She will take art class next year.

Adverbs

Write each adverb. Label the question it answers about the verb: **how, when,** or **where**.

1. Ava prepares carefully for the trip.
2. Her shoes are upstairs.
3. She quickly gets them.
4. Her mother often helps her pack.
5. The clothes are folded neatly.

More Practice

Prepositions of Place

Write the sentences. Underline the prepositions.

1. Put the crayons in the drawer.
2. The lamp is near the bookcase.
3. The paper is on the desk.
4. What is under the table?
5. The rug is under the table.

Conjunctions

Write each sentence. Underline the conjunctions.

1. The Alaskan tundra is a harsh and cold place.
2. The word *tundra* means "bare" or "treeless."
3. The Arctic fox and the Arctic wolf live in the tundra.
4. They have warm winter coats and bodies that hold heat.
5. Polar bears and penguins also live in the tundra.

More Practice

Its and It's

Write each sentence. Complete the sentence with **its** or **it's**.

1. The bird hurt ____ wing.
2. ____ going to need some food.
3. The vet will check ____ foot, too.
4. Dr. Chang thinks that ____ going to be okay.
5. It flew back up to ____ nest.

Irregular Verbs

Write each sentence. Complete the sentence with the past tense of the verb.

1. Dad (come) home in the afternoon.
2. He (give) us all presents.
3. He (say) he missed us.
4. I (wear) my new hat.
5. My sister (get) a new sweater.

More Practice

Compound Words

Write the compound words. Then write the words that make up the compound word.

1. Josh played the bagpipe.
2. Carlos skated downhill.
3. Rosa lost her earring.
4. Only Frank knows the password.
5. Mom carries a backpack.

Subject-Verb Agreement

Choose the verb that best completes each sentence. Write the sentences.

1. Brian and Lee (play/plays) together.
2. Brian (like/likes) hockey.
3. Lee (want/wants) a new hockey puck.
4. Brian (has/have) a new hockey stick.
5. Brian and Lee (need/needs) new uniforms.

More Practice

Comparing With Adjectives

Choose the adjective that best completes the sentence. Write the sentence.

1. My dog is (older/oldest) than your dog.
2. I ran my (faster/fastest) time ever today.
3. In my family, I have the (smaller/smallest) shoe size.
4. I am (bigger/biggest) than my best friend.
5. I am the (taller/tallest) student in my class.

Abbreviations

Write the words. Beside each word write the correct abbreviation.

1. Doctor
2. Thursday
3. September
4. Friday
5. January

More Practice

Contractions

Write the sentences. Replace the underlined word or words with the correct contraction.

1. I <u>was not</u> ready on time.
2. That <u>does not</u> matter.
3. I <u>cannot</u> wait to go.
4. I <u>have not</u> gone fishing for a long time.
5. I <u>did not</u> like boats.

Commas in a Series

Write the sentences. Underline the items in a series.

1. I packed shoes, shirts, and socks.
2. I need to bring a hat, a baseball, and a bat.
3. My mother, my sister, and my brother will help me.
4. Mike, Tony, and Jorge will share a tent.
5. They have sleeping bags, pillows, and blankets in the tent.

More Practice

Commas In Dates

Write each date. Add commas where they are needed.

1. February 14 2014
2. March 11 2012
3. October 17 2014
4. January 15 2013
5. May 2 1999

Parts of a Friendly Letter

Name the parts of a friendly letter.

1. What part shows the writer's address and date?
2. What part begins with Dear and ends with a comma?
3. What part tells the message?
4. What part ends the letter?
5. What part contains your name?

More Practice

Quotation Marks

Write the sentences. Put quotation marks before and after direct quotations.

1. Will you help me with my paper? Debbie asked.
2. Of course I will, said her mother.
3. Does Egypt sound like a good topic? Debbie asked.
4. Oh yes, it sounds like a great topic, her mother said.
5. I will also make a poster, Debbie told her mom.

Book Titles

Write the book titles correctly.

1. A Birthday basket for Tia
2. Alexander and the Wind-Up mouse
3. The seashore Book
4. nate the great
5. Ramona And beezus

Appendix B
Rubrics

4-Point Rubrics

5-Point Rubrics

6-Point Rubrics

Narrative Writing Rubric

	4	3	2	1
Ideas	The writing focuses on one story that covers a short period of time. Many details describe the setting and the actions, thoughts, and feelings of the characters.	The writing focuses on one story. Some details describe the setting and the actions, thoughts, and feelings of the characters.	The writing tells only part of a story, or it tells a story that is far too big to be told in detail. Few, if any, details describe the setting or the actions, thoughts, and feelings of the characters.	The writing does not tell a story. There is little or no detail.
Organization	Time-order words help the reader understand the storyline. The plot is easy to follow.	More or better time-order words would make the storyline clearer. The plot is not confusing.	Time-order words are missing or used incorrectly. The plot might be confusing or hard to follow.	No time-order words are used. There doesn't seem to be a plot.
Voice	The writer sounds interested in telling the story. If dialogue is used, characters sound like real people.	The writer sounds somewhat interested in telling the story. If dialogue is used, characters sound a little like real people.	It's hard to tell how the writer feels about writing the story. The writing lacks energy and personality. If dialogue is used, characters don't sound like real people.	The writer sounds bored. Dialogue is not used, or is very problematic.
Word Choice	The story is written with unique and specific words that help bring the story to life. Adjectives and adverbs are strong.	The story is written with clear wording. Adjectives and adverbs are used.	The words of the story are not specific. Adjectives and adverbs are missing or weak.	Many words are used incorrectly. Adjectives and adverbs are not used.
Sentence Fluency	Most of the sentences are different lengths. Compound sentences are used. Most sentences begin with different words.	Some sentences are different lengths. A compound sentence might be used. Some sentences begin with different words.	Many sentences are about the same length. Many sentences begin with the same words. The writing doesn't flow very well.	Many sentences are fragments or run-ons, or are written incorrectly.
Conventions	There are only a few mistakes in capitalization, punctuation, or spelling. The writing is legible and easy to read.	There are some mistakes in capitalization, punctuation, or spelling. The writing is somewhat legible and easy to read.	There are many mistakes in capitalization, punctuation, and spelling. Mistakes and/or poor handwriting make the paper difficult to read.	The writing has not been edited. It is very hard to read.

Informative/Explanatory Writing Rubric

	4	3	2	1
Ideas	The topic is introduced very clearly and developed with many interesting details.	The topic is introduced and developed with enough details.	The reader may have to guess what the topic is. There are few details, and some may be incorrect.	The topic is not introduced. Details are not provided.
Organization	The writing has an introduction, a body, and a conclusion. Nothing is out of place. Good time-order words connect the ideas.	The writing has an introduction, a body, and a conclusion. Ideas go together in a way that makes sense. Some time-order words are used.	The writing may be missing an introduction, a conclusion, or both. Some ideas may be out of place. Time-order words are missing or incorrect.	The writing is very poorly organized and hard to follow.
Voice	The writer sounds interested and knowledgeable. The writing is respectful without sounding too formal or stiff.	The writer sounds somewhat interested and knowledgeable. Much of the writing is respectful. A few places may sound stiff or too informal.	It's hard to tell how much the writer knows or cares about the topic. The writing may sound too stiff in some places or too informal in other places.	The writer is obviously bored and is not knowledgeable about the topic. The reader is bored, too.
Word Choice	Topic-related words are used effectively. Words that the reader might not know are explained.	Topic-related words are used. Some unknown words are explained for the reader.	Few topic-related words are used correctly. Explanations of unknown words are missing or confusing.	Words are chosen very poorly. Many words are used incorrectly.
Sentence Fluency	Most sentences begin with different words. Many sentences are different lengths. Compound sentences are used.	Some sentences begin in different ways. Some sentences are different lengths. Compound sentences might be used.	Most sentences begin with the same words. Most sentences are about the same length.	Many sentences are written incorrectly. There may be many fragments or run-ons.
Conventions	There are only a few mistakes in capitalization, punctuation, or spelling. The writing is legible and easy to read.	There are some mistakes in capitalization, punctuation, or spelling. The writing is somewhat legible and easy to read.	There are many mistakes in capitalization, punctuation, and spelling. Mistakes and/or poor handwriting make the paper difficult to read.	The writing has not been edited. It is very hard to read.

Opinion Writing Rubric

	4	3	2	1
Ideas	The writer's opinion is very clear. Specific reasons and examples are given.	The writer's opinion is clear. Reasons and some examples are given.	The writer's opinion is not clear. Reasons are not convincing or don't make sense. Specific examples are not given.	The writer's opinion cannot be determined.
Organization	The writing has an introduction and a conclusion. Reasons and examples are grouped into a body that makes sense. Many linking words are used to connect the reasons and examples.	The writing has an introduction and a conclusion. Reasons and examples are grouped into a body that mostly makes sense. Some linking words are used to connect the reasons and examples.	The writing may be missing an introduction, a conclusion, or both. Some reasons are grouped into a body, but they may be disorganized. Few, if any, linking words are used.	The writing is very poorly organized and hard to follow.
Voice	The writer sounds convincing most of the time. The point of view is consistent. The writing is mostly respectful without sounding too formal or stiff.	The writer sounds convincing some of the time. The point of view is somewhat consistent. Much of the writing is respectful. A few places may sound stiff or too informal.	The writer does not sound convincing. The point of view shifts. The writing may sound too stiff in some places or too informal in other places.	The writer does not express an opinion. The point of view cannot be determined.
Word Choice	Most of the writer's words, including adjectives and adverbs, are precise and give a clear message.	Some of the words, including adjectives and adverbs, are precise. The message is clear.	Many words are vague or unclear. The message may be hard to understand.	Many words are used incorrectly. The message is not clear.
Sentence Fluency	Most sentence structures are varied and interesting. Compound sentences are used.	Some of the sentence structures are varied and interesting. A compound sentence may be used.	Most sentences share the same structure.	Sentences are fragments or run-ons, or are written incorrectly
Conventions	There are only a few mistakes in capitalization, punctuation, or spelling. The writing is legible and easy to read.	There are some mistakes in capitalization, punctuation, or spelling. The writing is somewhat legible and easy to read.	There are many mistakes in capitalization, punctuation, and spelling. Mistakes and/or poor handwriting make the paper difficult to read.	The writing has not been edited. It is very hard to read.

Descriptive Writing Rubric

	4	3	2	1
Ideas	The topic is clear and focused. Many details describe and develop the topic. A simile (or other figurative language) may be used to clarify ideas.	The topic is somewhat clear and focused. Some details develop the topic. A simile (or other figurative language) may be used.	The topic needs to be more focused. Too few descriptive details develop the topic.	A topic is not clearly introduced. Details are missing or unrelated to the topic.
Organization	The description is well organized and easy to follow. Transition words guide the reader.	Some of the description is organized. Transition words are used correctly.	Most of the description is not organized. More or better transitions are needed.	The writing is not a description. A few details are listed but are not organized.
Voice	The voice engages the audience. It's clear the writer likes writing about the topic.	The voice engages the audience some of the time. The writer shows some interest in the topic.	The voice does not engage the audience. The writer's interest in the topic is not clear.	The voice is weak. The writer is bored, and so is the reader.
Word Choice	Nouns and verbs are specific. Strong adjectives, adverbs, and descriptive phrases are used.	Some nouns and verbs are specific. Some adjectives, adverbs, and descriptive phrases are used.	Many words are vague or general. Few, if any, adjectives, adverbs, or descriptive phrases are used.	Many words are not used correctly.
Sentence Fluency	Most sentence structures and lengths are varied. Compound sentences are used.	Some sentence structures and lengths are varied. A compound sentence may be used.	Too many sentences share the same structure or length.	Sentences are fragments or run-ons, or are written incorrectly.
Conventions	There are only a few mistakes in capitalization, punctuation, or spelling. The writing is legible and easy to read.	There are some mistakes in capitalization, punctuation, or spelling. The writing is somewhat legible and easy to read.	There are many mistakes in capitalization, punctuation, and spelling. Mistakes and/or poor handwriting make the paper difficult to read.	The writing has not been edited. It is very hard to read.

Narrative Writing Rubric

	5	4	3	2	1
Ideas	The writing focuses very clearly on one story that covers a short period of time. Many strong details describe the setting. Strong details also describe the actions, thoughts, and feelings of the characters.	The writing focuses on one story that covers a short period of time. Many details describe the setting and the actions, thoughts, and feelings of the characters.	The writing focuses on one story. Some details describe the setting and the actions, thoughts, and feelings of the characters.	The writing tells only part of a story, or it tells a story that is far too big to be told in detail. Few, if any, details describe the setting or the actions, thoughts, and feelings of the characters.	The writing does not tell a story. There is little or no detail.
Organization	Strong or unique time-order words are used. The plot makes perfect sense.	Time-order words help the reader understand the storyline. The plot is easy to follow.	More or better time-order words would make the storyline clearer. The plot is not confusing.	Time-order words are missing or used incorrectly. The plot might be confusing.	No time-order words are used. There doesn't seem to be a plot.
Voice	The writer sounds very interested in telling the story. If dialogue is used, characters sound exactly like real people.	The writer sounds interested in telling the story. If dialogue is used, characters sound mostly like real people.	The writer sounds somewhat interested in telling the story. If dialogue is used, characters sound a little like real people.	It's hard to tell how the writer feels about writing the story. The writing lacks energy and personality. If dialogue is used, characters don't sound like real people.	The writer sounds bored. Dialogue is not used, or is very problematic.
Word Choice	The writing is full of unique and specific words that bring the story to life. Adjectives and adverbs are very strong.	The story is written with specific words that help bring the story to life in some places. Adjectives and adverbs are good.	The story is written with clear wording. Adjectives and adverbs are used.	The words of the story are not specific. Adjectives and adverbs are missing or weak.	Many words are used incorrectly. Adjectives and adverbs are not used.
Sentence Fluency	Most sentences are different lengths. Compound sentences are used very effectively. Almost all sentences begin with different words.	Many of the sentences are different lengths. Compound sentences are used. Most sentences begin with different words.	Some of the sentences are different lengths. A compound sentence might be used. Some sentences begin with different words.	Many sentences are about the same length. Many sentences begin with the same words. The writing doesn't flow very well.	Many sentences are fragments or run-ons, or are written incorrectly.
Conventions	There are no mistakes in capitalization, punctuation, or spelling. The writing is legible and easy to read.	There are only a few mistakes in capitalization, punctuation, or spelling. The writing is mostly legible and easy to read.	There are some mistakes in capitalization, punctuation, or spelling. The writing is somewhat legible and easy to read.	There are many mistakes in capitalization, punctuation, and spelling. Mistakes and/or poor handwriting make the paper difficult to read.	The writing has not been edited. It is very hard to read.

Informative/Explanatory Writing Rubric

	5	4	3	2	1
Ideas	The topic is introduced very clearly and is developed with many interesting details.	The topic is introduced and developed with interesting details.	The topic is introduced and developed with enough details.	The reader may have to guess what the topic is. There are few details, and some may be incorrect.	The topic is not clearly introduced. Details are not provided.
Organization	The writing has a clear introduction, body, and conclusion. Nothing is out of place. Many good time-order words clearly connect ideas.	The writing has an introduction, a body, and a conclusion. Almost nothing is out of place.Good time-order words connect the ideas.	The writing has an introduction, a body, and a conclusion. Ideas go together in a way that makes sense. Some time-order words are used.	The writing may be missing an introduction, a conclusion, or both. Some ideas might be out of place. Time-order words are missing or incorrect.	The writing is very poorly organized and hard to follow.
Voice	The writer sounds very interested and knowledgeable. The writing is always respectful without sounding too formal or stiff.	The writer sounds interested and knowledgeable. The writing is mostly respectful without sounding stiff.	The writer sounds somewhat interested and knowledgeable. Much of the writing is respectful. A few places may sound too stiff or too informal.	It's hard to tell how much the author knows or cares about the topic. The writing sounds too stiff in some places or too informal in other places.	The writer is obviously bored and not knowledgeable about the topic. The reader is bored, too.
Word Choice	Many topic-related words are used very effectively. All words that the reader might not know are explained.	Topic-related words are used effectively. Words that the reader doesn't know are usually explained.	Topic-related words are used. Some unknown words are explained for the reader.	Few topic-related words are used correctly. Explanations of unknown words are missing or confusing.	Words are chosen very poorly. Many words are used incorrectly.
Sentence Fluency	Almost all sentences begin with different words. Almost all sentences vary in length. Compound sentences are used very effectively.	Many sentences begin with different words. Many sentences are different lengths. Compound sentences are used.	Some sentences begin in different ways. Some sentences are different lengths. Compound sentences might be used.	Most sentences begin with the same words. Most sentences are about the same length.	Many sentences are written incorrectly. There may be many fragments or run-ons.
Conventions	There are no mistakes in capitalization, punctuation, or spelling. The writing is legible and easy to read.	There are only a few mistakes in capitalization, punctuation, or spelling. The writing is mostly legible and easy to read.	There are some mistakes in capitalization, punctuation, or spelling. The writing is somewhat legible and easy to read.	There are many mistakes in capitalization, punctuation, and spelling. Mistakes and/ or poor handwriting make the paper difficult to read.	The writing has not been edited. It is very hard to read.

Opinion Writing Rubric

	5	4	3	2	1
Ideas	The writer's opinion is very clear. Convincing reasons and strong examples are given.	The writer's opinion is clear. Reasons and some specific examples are given.	The writer's opinion is clear. Reasons and some examples are given.	The writer's opinion is not clear. Reasons are not given or don't make sense. Specific examples are not given.	The writer's opinion cannot be determined.
Organization	The writing has a clear introduction and conclusion. Reasons and examples are grouped into a body that makes sense. Many linking words are used effectively to connect the reasons and examples.	The writing has an introduction and a conclusion. Reasons and examples are grouped into a body that makes sense. Many linking words are used to connect the reasons and examples.	The writing has an introduction and a conclusion. Reasons and examples are grouped into a body that mostly makes sense. Some linking words are used to connect the reasons and examples.	The writing may be missing an introduction, a conclusion, or both. Some reasons are grouped into a body, but they may be disorganized. Few, if any, linking words are used.	The writing is very poorly organized and hard to follow.
Voice	The writer sounds very convincing. The point of view is clear and consistent. The writing is respectful without sounding too formal or stiff.	The writer sounds convincing most of the time. The point of view is mostly consistent. The writing is mostly respectful without sounding stiff.	The writer sounds convincing some of the time. The point of view is somewhat consistent. Much of the writing is respectful. A few places may sound too stiff or too informal.	The writer does not sound convincing. The point of view shifts. The writing sounds too stiff or too informal.	The writer does not express an opinion. The point of view cannot be determined.
Word Choice	The writer uses precise, well-chosen words (especially adjectives and adverbs) that give a clear message.	Many of the writer's words, including adjectives and adverbs, are precise and give a clear message.	Some of the words, including adjectives and adverbs, are precise. The message is clear.	Many words are vague or unclear. The message may be hard to understand.	Many words are used incorrectly. The message is not clear.
Sentence Fluency	Sentence structures are varied and interesting, including effective compound sentences.	Most sentence structures are varied and interesting. Compound sentences are used.	Some of the sentence structures are varied and interesting. A compound sentence may be used.	Most sentences share the same structure.	Sentences are fragments or run-ons, or are written incorrectly.
Conventions	There are no mistakes in capitalization, punctuation, or spelling. The writing is very legible and easy to read.	There are only a few mistakes in capitalization, punctuation, or spelling. The writing is legible and easy to read.	There are some mistakes in capitalization, punctuation, or spelling. The writing is somewhat legible and easy to read.	There are many mistakes in capitalization, punctuation, and spelling. Mistakes and/or poor handwriting make the paper difficult to read.	The writing has not been edited. It is very hard to read.

Descriptive Writing Rubric

	5	4	3	2	1
Ideas	The topic is very clear, focused, and interesting. Many sensory details describe and develop the topic. Similes (or other figurative language) may be used to clarify ideas.	The topic is mostly clear and focused. Many details describe and develop the topic. A simile (or other figurative language) may be used to clarify ideas.	The topic is somewhat clear and focused. Some details develop the topic. A simile (or other figurative language) may be used.	The topic needs to be more focused. Too few descriptive details develop the topic.	A topic is not clearly introduced. Details are missing or unrelated to the topic.
Organization	The description is very well organized and easy to follow. Strong, helpful transition words guide the reader.	Much of the description is organized. Transition words guide the reader.	Some of the description is organized. Transition words are used.	Most of the description is not organized. More or better transitions are needed.	The writing is not a description. A few details are listed but not organized.
Voice	The voice strongly engages the audience. It's clear the writer likes writing about the topic and wants to share it with the reader.	The voice engages the audience most of the time. It's clear the writer likes writing about the topic.	The voice engages the audience some of the time. The writer shows interest in the topic.	The voice does not engage the audience. The writer's interest in the topic is not clear.	The voice is weak. The writer is bored, and so is the reader.
Word Choice	Nouns and verbs are very specific. Many strong adjectives, adverbs, and descriptive phrases are used.	Nouns and verbs are specific. Adjectives, adverbs, and descriptive phrases are used.	Some nouns and verbs are specific. Some adjectives, adverbs, and descriptive phrases are used.	Many words are vague or general. Few, if any, adjectives, adverbs, or descriptive phrases are used.	Many words are not used correctly.
Sentence Fluency	A wide variety of sentence patterns and lengths makes the description flow very well. Compound sentences are used very effectively.	Most sentence structures and lengths are varied. Compound sentences are used.	Some sentence structures and lengths are varied. A compound sentence may be used.	Too many sentences share the same structure or length.	Sentences are fragments or run-ons, or are written incorrectly.
Conventions	There are no mistakes in capitalization, punctuation, or spelling. The writing is legible and easy to read.	There are only a few mistakes in capitalization, punctuation, or spelling. The writing is mostly legible and easy to read.	There are some mistakes in capitalization, punctuation, or spelling. The writing is some-what legible and easy to read.	There are many mistakes in capitalization, punctuation, and spelling. Mistakes and/ or poor handwriting make the paper difficult to read.	The writing has not been edited. It is very hard to read.

Narrative Writing Rubric

	6	5	4	3	2	1
Ideas	The writing focuses very clearly on one story that covers a short period of time. Many strong details describe the setting and the actions, thoughts, and feelings of the characters.	The writing focuses on one story that covers a short period of time. Many details describe the setting and the actions, thoughts, and feelings of the characters.	The writing focuses on one story. Some details describe the setting and the actions, thoughts, and feelings of the characters.	The writing focuses on one story, but the story is too big to be told in detail. Few details describe the setting or the actions, thoughts, and feelings of the characters.	The writing tells only part of a story, or it tells a story that is far too big to be told in detail. Details are weak, unrelated, or missing.	The writing does not tell a story. There is little or no detail.
Organization	Strong or unique time-order words are used. The plot makes perfect sense.	Time-order words help the reader understand the storyline. The plot is easy to follow.	More or better time-order words would make the storyline clearer. The plot is not confusing.	There are only one or two time-order words. The plot is hard to follow in one or two places.	Time-order words are missing or used incorrectly. The plot is confusing.	No time-order words are used. There doesn't seem to be a plot.
Voice	The writer sounds very interested in telling the story. If dialogue is used, characters sound exactly like real people.	The writer sounds interested in telling the story. If dialogue is used, characters sound mostly like real people.	The writer sounds somewhat interested in telling the story. If dialogue is used, characters sound a little like real people.	It's hard to tell how the writer feels about writing the story. The writing lacks energy and personality. If dialogue is used, characters don't sound like real people.	The writer doesn't sound interested in telling the story. If dialogue is used, it's hard to understand what characters are saying.	The writer sounds bored. Dialogue is not used, or is very problematic.
Word Choice	The writing is full of unique and specific words that bring the story to life. Adjectives and adverbs are very strong.	The story is written with specific words that help bring the story to life in some places. Adjectives and adverbs are strong.	The story is written with clear wording. Adjectives and adverbs are used.	The words of the story are not very specific. Adjectives and adverbs are weak.	The words of the story are boring or vague. Adjectives and adverbs are missing or very weak.	Many words are used incorrectly. Adjectives and adverbs are not used.
Sentence Fluency	Most sentences are different lengths. Compound sentences are used very effectively. Almost all sentences begin with different words.	Many of the sentences are different lengths. Compound sentences are used. Most sentences begin with different words.	Some of the sentences are different lengths. A compound sentence might be used. Some sentences begin with different words.	Many sentences are about the same length. Many sentences begin with the same words. The writing doesn't flow very well.	Almost all of the sentences are the same length. Almost all sentences start with the same words.	Many sentences are fragments or run-ons, or are written incorrectly.
Conventions	There are no mistakes in capitalization, punctuation, or spelling. The writing is completely legible and easy to read.	There are only a few mistakes in capitalization, punctuation, or spelling. The writing is mostly legible and easy to read.	There are some mistakes in capitalization, punctuation, or spelling. The writing is somewhat legible and easy to read.	There are mistakes in capitalization, punctuation, and spelling. Mistakes and/or poor handwriting make the paper difficult to read.	There are many mistakes in capitalization, punctuation, and spelling. Mistakes and/or poor handwriting cause confusion for the reader.	The writing has not been edited. It is very hard to read.

Informative/Explanatory Writing Rubric

	6	5	4	3	2	1
Ideas	The topic is introduced very clearly and developed with many interesting details.	The topic is introduced and developed with some interesting details.	The topic is introduced and developed with enough details.	The topic is introduced, but not enough details are given to develop it.	The reader may have to guess what the topic is. Details are missing or are incorrect.	The topic is not introduced. Details are not provided.
Organization	The writing has a clear introduction, body, and conclusion. Nothing is out of place. Many good time-order words or other transitions clearly connect ideas.	The writing has an introduction, a body, and a conclusion. Almost nothing is out of place. Good time-order words or other transitions connect the ideas.	The writing has an introduction, a body, and a conclusion. Ideas go together in a way that makes sense. Some time-order words or other transitions are used.	The writing may be missing an introduction or a conclusion. Some ideas are out of place. Few time-order words or other transitions are used.	The writing does not have an introduction or a conclusion. Transition words are missing or incorrect.	The writing is very poorly organized and hard to follow.
Voice	The writer sounds very interested and knowledgeable. The writing is always respectful without sounding too formal or stiff.	The writer sounds interested and knowledgeable. The writing is mostly respectful without sounding stiff.	The writer sounds somewhat interested and knowledgeable. Much of the writing is respectful. A few places may sound too stiff or too informal.	It's hard to tell how much the author knows or cares about the topic. The writing sounds too stiff in some places or too informal in other places.	The writer doesn't sound interested or knowledgeable. Much of the writing sounds too stiff or too informal.	The writer is obviously bored and is not knowledgeable about the topic. The reader is bored, too.
Word Choice	Many topic-related words are used very effectively. All words that the reader might not know are explained.	Topic-related words are used effectively. Words that the reader doesn't know are usually explained.	Topic-related words are used. Some unknown words are explained for the reader.	Few topic-related words are used, and they may need to be explained better.	Topic-related words are not used correctly. Explanations are confusing or incorrect.	Words are chosen very poorly. Many words are used incorrectly.
Sentence Fluency	Almost all sentences begin with different words. Almost all sentences vary in length. Compound sentences are used very effectively.	Many sentences begin with different words. Many sentences are different lengths. Compound sentences are used.	Some sentences begin in different ways. Some sentences are different lengths. A compound sentence might be used.	Many sentences begin with the same words, and many are about the same length.	Most sentences begin with the same words. Most sentences are about the same length.	Many sentences are written incorrectly. There may be many fragments or run-ons.
Conventions	There are no mistakes in capitalization, punctuation, or spelling. The writing is completely legible and easy to read.	There are only a few mistakes in capitalization, punctuation, or spelling. The writing is mostly legible and easy to read.	There are some mistakes in capitalization, punctuation, or spelling. The writing is somewhat legible and easy to read.	There are mistakes in capitalization, punctuation, and spelling. Mistakes and/or poor handwriting make the paper difficult to read.	There are many mistakes in capitalization, punctuation, and spelling. Mistakes and/or poor handwriting cause confusion for the reader.	The writing has not been edited. It is very hard to read.

Opinion Writing Rubric

	6	5	4	3	2	1
Ideas	The writer's opinion is very clear. Convincing reasons and strong examples are given.	The writer's opinion is clear. Reasons and some specific examples are given.	The writer's opinion is clear. Reasons and some examples are given.	The writer's opinion is fairly clear. A few reasons are given, but specific examples may not be given.	The writer's opinion is not very clear. Reasons are not given or don't make sense.	The writer's opinion cannot be determined.
Organization	The writing has a clear introduction and conclusion. Reasons and examples are grouped into a body that makes sense. Many linking words are used effectively to connect the reasons and examples.	The writing has an introduction and a conclusion. Reasons and examples are grouped into a body that mostly makes sense. Many linking words are used to connect the reasons and examples.	The writing has an introduction and a conclusion. Reasons and examples are grouped into a body that mostly makes sense. Some linking words are used to connect the reasons and examples.	The writing may be missing an introduction or a conclusion. Some reasons are grouped into a body. Few linking words are used.	The writing does not have an introduction or a conclusion. Reasons are missing or disorganized. Linking words are missing or used incorrectly.	The writing is very poorly organized and hard to follow.
Voice	The writer sounds very convincing. The point of view is clear and consistent. The writing is respectful without sounding too formal or stiff.	The writer sounds convincing most of the time. The point of view is mostly consistent. The writing is mostly respectful without sounding stiff.	The writer sounds convincing some of the time. The point of view is somewhat consistent. Much of the writing is respectful. A few places may sound too stiff or informal.	The writer isn't very convincing. The point of view may shift. The writing may sound too stiff in some places or too informal in other places.	The writer does not sound convincing. The point of view changes a lot. The writing sounds too stiff or too informal.	The writer does not express an opinion. The point of view cannot be determined.
Word Choice	The writer uses precise, well-chosen words (especially adjectives and adverbs) that give a clear message.	Many of the writer's words, including adjectives and adverbs, are precise and give a clear message.	Some words, including adjectives and adverbs, are precise. The message is clear.	Many words are vague or poorly chosen. The message may be confusing in parts.	Many vague or unclear words make most of the message hard to understand.	Many words are used incorrectly. The message is not clear.
Sentence Fluency	Sentence structures are varied and interesting, including compound sentences.	Many sentence structures are varied and interesting. Compound sentences are used.	Some of the sentence structures are varied and interesting. A compound sentence may be used.	Many sentences share the same structure.	All sentences share a similar structure.	Sentences are fragments or run-ons, or are written incorrectly.
Conventions	There are no mistakes in capitalization, punctuation, or spelling. The writing is very legible and easy to read.	There are only a few mistakes in capitalization, punctuation, or spelling. The writing is legible and easy to read.	There are some mistakes in capitalization, punctuation, or spelling. The writing is somewhat legible and easy to read.	There are mistakes in capitalization, punctuation, and spelling. Mistakes and/or poor handwriting make the paper difficult to read.	There are many mistakes in capitalization, punctuation, and spelling. Mistakes and/or poor handwriting cause confusion for the reader.	The writing has not been edited. It is very hard to read.

Descriptive Writing Rubric

	6	5	4	3	2	1
Ideas	The topic is very clear, focused, and interesting. Many sensory details describe and develop the topic. Similes (or other figurative language) may be used to clarify ideas.	The topic is mostly clear and focused. Many details describe and develop the topic. A simile (or other figurative language) may be used to clarify ideas.	The topic is somewhat clear and focused. Some details develop the topic. A simile (or other figurative language) may be used.	The topic is clear but needs to be more focused. Too few descriptive details develop the topic.	A topic may be inferred. Details are not descriptive.	A topic is not clearly introduced. Details are missing or unrelated to the topic.
Organization	The description is very well organized and easy to follow. Strong, helpful transition words guide the reader.	The description is organized. Transition words guide the reader.	Most of the description is organized. Transition words are used.	Some of the description is organized. More or better transitions are needed.	Most of the description is not organized. Transition words are not used.	The writing is not a description. A few details are listed but not organized.
Voice	The voice strongly engages the audience. It's clear the writer likes writing about the topic and wants to share it with the reader.	The voice engages the audience most of the time. It's clear the writer likes writing about the topic.	The voice engages the audience some of the time. The writer shows interest in the topic.	The voice rarely engages the audience. The writer's interest in the topic is not clear.	The voice does not engage the audience. The writer does not show interest in the topic.	The voice is weak. The writer is bored, and so is the reader.
Word Choice	Nouns and verbs are very specific. Many strong adjectives, adverbs, and descriptive phrases are used.	Nouns and verbs are specific. Many adjectives, adverbs, and descriptive phrases are used.	Some nouns and verbs are specific. Some adjectives, adverbs, and descriptive phrases are used.	Many words are vague or general. Few adjectives, adverbs, or descriptive phrases are used.	Few words describe the topic. No adjectives, adverbs, or descriptive phrases are used.	Many words are not used correctly.
Sentence Fluency	A wide variety of sentence patterns and lengths make the description flow well. Compound sentences are used effectively.	Most sentence structures and lengths are varied. Compound sentences are used.	Some sentence structures and lengths are varied. A compound sentence may be used.	Too many sentences share the same structure or length.	All of the sentences share the same structure and length.	Sentences are fragments or run-ons, or are written incorrectly.
Conventions	There are no mistakes in capitalization, punctuation, or spelling. The writing is very legible and easy to read.	There are only a few mistakes in capitalization, punctuation, or spelling. The writing is mostly legible and easy to read.	There are some mistakes in capitalization, punctuation, or spelling. The writing is somewhat legible and easy to read.	There are mistakes in capitalization, punctuation, and spelling. Mistakes and/or poor handwriting make the paper difficult to read.	There are many mistakes in capitalization, punctuation, and spelling. Mistakes and/or poor handwriting cause confusion for the reader.	The writing has not been edited. It is very hard to read.

Index

H

I